# teaching
## third edition

## from the inside out

**Larry Beauchamp
and Jim Parsons**

DUVAL HOUSE
PUBLISHING

Third Edition 5 4 3 2 1

copyright © 2000 Les Editions Duval, Inc.

Duval House Publishing/Les Editions Duval, Inc.

Head Office:
18228 - 102 Avenue
Edmonton, Alberta
CANADA  T5S 1S7
Telephone: (780) 482-4845
Fax: (780) 482-7213
Toll-free: 1-800-267-6187
E-mail: pdr@compusmart.ab.ca
Website: www.duvalhouse.com

Ontario Office:
5 Graham Avenue
Ottawa, Ontario
CANADA  K1S 0B6
Telephone: (613) 237-0305
Fax: (613) 237-0306
Toll-free: 1-800-597-0323
E-mail: 3jp@compuserve.com

Typeset by Pièce de Résistance Ltée.
Printed and bound in Canada by Quality Color Press.

 We acknowledge the financial support of the Government of Canada through the Book Publishing Industry Development Program (BPIDP) for our publishing activities.

**Canadian Cataloguing in Publication Data**

Beauchamp, Larry, 1943–
   Teaching from the inside out

   Includes index.
   ISBN 1-55220-106-6

   1. Teaching.  I. Parsons, Jim, 1948–  II. Title.

LB1025.3.B43 2000   371.102   C00-910855-6

# Contents

## SECTION THREE

# Preface

We started this preface with a quote. As you read the book you will notice that we have included many more in the body of the text. We hope these quotes will enrich what you are reading. We intend them to give you reason to pause and explore alternative points of view. We mean to encourage you to discuss these quotes with fellow students, teachers, friends or anyone else who will engage you. From our point of view, the ambiguity and contradiction suggested in many of the quotes is not problematic. We hope it will push you toward a problem-solving or problem-posing approach to learning.

We have included a brief annotated bibliography at the end of each chapter. These readings are intended for extension and enrichment. As such, they do not necessarily espouse the same concepts or philosophy prevalent in the chapter. We hope these readings will provide alternative points of view to stimulate your thinking as you develop and refine your own positions on each of the chapter topics.

This book was designed to help you develop a sense of what teaching is really about. You can read textbooks and journals, but will they help you survive and flourish as a beginning teacher? You can piece together psychology, historical foundations to education, and principles of planning and motivation; but will your work give you the kind of advice you need to get out there and teach? This book is intended to share the wisdom of teaching in a very practical way. It reviews problems that you will undoubtedly face as a teacher and offers you some insight into how to address these problems by yourself.

Most education textbooks we read are heavy on intellect, but low on passion. They lack the Renaissance mentality of combining the will and the intellect. They are encyclopedic and seem to be afraid to take a stand. In this book we have tried to identify with the reader, rely on good experience, and make claims. We hope, by the time you finish reading this book, you will realize just how much we love teaching. We also hope that you will find that we did what we set out to do: to celebrate teaching and make a positive move toward a restoration of pride in teaching.

We are not sure if we succeeded in what we set out to do. Only you, the reader, can inform us. We encourage you to write to us, and we look forward to any response you might have.

Larry Beauchamp
Jim Parsons
Department of Secondary Education
University of Alberta.

# Dedication: To the Memory of Rachel Emily Germaine

On June 6, 1993, a baby was born and died in Red Deer, Alberta. The baby's name was Rachel. Rachel's mother is a biology teacher. Her life as a teacher is ever altered by her love for her baby and the brief memories they shared together.

We want to dedicate this book to the truth that every single human life is a delicate treasure to be cared for and nourished. Every single child in every single classroom is a sacred trust given to teachers. This is the single, most important fact that a good teacher must learn. It is for the millions of Rachels in classrooms everywhere that we wrote this book.

# Thank You

We wish to thank the following people for their contributions to this book. We thank Gerry McConaghy for his continued support of the need for this book, for his rigorous editing, and for the hundreds of practical things he did that aided the production of the book. We also thank Kathy Smith for her gentle but "in-your-face" persuasiveness that was the impetus for changes that, although they would not have happened otherwise, have proved to be exceptionally insightful and positive. We also wish to thank those teachers, Nick Forsberg and Louise Humbert, who used first-draft copies of the book in their classes. We also wish to thank Dawn Ford for her numerous suggestions, all of which we incorporated, for improving the substance and quality of this third edition.

*WHAT does education often do? It makes a straight-cut ditch of a free meandering brook.*

**- HENRY DAVID THOREAU**

You have chosen to pursue a career in which you have much previous knowledge and experience. After all, you have probably been a student for the past 12 or more years. The purpose of this first section is to help you recall such experience and knowledge and to put it into a framework that will help you as you prepare to become a teacher. Why do you want to teach? Why do teachers like their jobs? What are your students' needs? Why can't all students succeed? How should you interact with students? With colleagues? With administrators? With parents? How can you establish authority in your classroom? What is the difference between punishment and discipline? These are but a few of the questions that will be addressed in this section.

LAYING THE GROUNDWORK

# CHAPTER 1

# Why Do You Want to Teach?

*TEACHING is a lonely enterprise. Physicians confer over patient diagnoses; prosecution and defense attorneys rehash trials; professional athletes study videotapes of their competitors; artists scrutinize each other's canvases; and writers habitually review the work of their colleagues. Teachers, in contrast, function in professional quarantine, rarely having the opportunity to observe other classrooms, compare beliefs, exchange views, and consider options. It is hardly surprising, then, that so many suffer a crippled spirit.*

**- L. RUBIN**

## INTRODUCTION

Why, you ask, did these writers start with such a quote? Are they trying to scare me off? Our answer is that we want people who are going to become teachers to think seriously about what it means to be a teacher. We don't mean to scare off anyone who would be a good teacher, but we do want to scare off those people who are in teaching for a cake walk. Or because they can think of nothing better to do. We want to encourage those who really want to be teachers.

We are going to begin our book with maybe the most important question we can ask: *Why do you want to become a teacher?* Were you encouraged by the good example of a positive model, a teacher whom you wanted to be like? Or, as many of our students tell us, were you encouraged to become a teacher because the teachers you had were so dreadfully awful? Did you want to prove to them (at least figuratively) that it was possible to be a good teacher no matter how hard they tried to prove the opposite?

One of the things that you will find as you read this book is that we like to tell you about "the research." Teaching is an area where there has been quite a bit of research. As a result, we know some things about how classrooms work, how teachers think, and how students behave.

We also read the research to help us try to solve problems that teachers come across. While the research doesn't always give direct answers, it does offer ideas that provide hints about what we might do or what we probably shouldn't do.

In a way this is a book of teaching hints. We are writing it because we are trying our best to help you become good teachers. We don't know all the answers, but we do know some of them. We have learned some things that have worked for us. We have spent time talking to teachers, both those who are successful and those who aren't. And we have read the research (there's that phrase again). We hope that this book saves you some grief. We hope that thinking about some of the things we say will keep you from making some of the same teaching mistakes we made. If we can, we want to keep you out of trouble—to try to make teaching easier.

We know that teaching has good and bad parts, and we want you to get to the good parts just as fast as you can. We don't mean to scare you again, but you should know that teaching is not always easy. (Tell us something new, you say.)

## WHY DO YOU WANT TO TEACH?

Now that we have told you that we have read the research, let's tell you some of the things it says. Overall, when asked "Why do you want to teach?" student responses fall into five categories. These are the categories, in order of choice:

1) I like children. I want to help them and work with them. Teaching gives me this opportunity. (interpersonal theme)
2) There are some material benefits including money, prestige, status, and security that I couldn't get anywhere else. (material benefits theme)
3) I want to remain in a school setting or I am interested in a subject. (continuation theme)
4) Teaching is a valuable service of special moral worth. (service theme)
5) I like having the summer off and all the holiday breaks. (flexibility theme)

## WHY DID WE BECOME TEACHERS, AND WHY DO WE LIKE THE JOB?

Throughout the remainder of this book, we will be pressing you to answer some questions about why you want to become a teacher. We will be telling you how important we think it is to reflect on and consider your decision very carefully. We will be asking you all sorts of personal questions because we believe that pushing the questions we ask is important.

We talked about different ways of putting this book together, and we decided that it would only be fair, if we were going to ask you difficult questions, that we answer some of these questions ourselves. The rest of this chapter talks about why we became teachers and why we like being teachers.

### JIM

I have a friend and colleague in social studies named Joe Kirman. Joe and I talk about many things,

**"We are our choices."**
*- Jean Paul Sartre*

one of them being religious beliefs. Joe, who is Jewish, tells me that there is an old Jewish belief that when Jewish people die and go to face God to discuss their lives they are asked two questions. Question one is "Did you take advantage of all the rightful pleasures that I created for you?" If they answer no, they are made to say why. Question two is "Did you believe that I created the world just for you?" The reasoning behind this question is that if people believe that God created the world just for them, they will have a special appreciation of life.

I believe that God created teaching just for me! I can't think of anything that I would rather do. Most days I love going to work. In fact, the only thing I dislike about teaching is grading a huge pile of assignments, especially the same thing repeatedly.

When I was a real teacher, and not a university professor, I taught grade seven. It was the only grade I ever taught, although I later substitute taught in both elementary and senior high schools.

I never started out to be a teacher. I graduated from the University of Kentucky in psychology, but when a new program developed to help find teachers for the city schools in Louisville, I quickly decided that I didn't want to be a psychologist. Instead, it seemed that it might be more fun to work with young people. In the summer before school started, I took three education courses (one in general curriculum, one in children's literature, and one in educational foundations). I was pronounced fit for service starting in September.

I never did student teach; I never even saw a student teacher work. My first day in front of a class, ever, was the first day of my first year teaching. I was really bad. I was so bad that I decided that I would set my sights low. I vowed that my students would have at least ten positive educational experiences that year. Fortunately, the number ten corresponded to the number of times that I could have a substitute teacher.

I made it through the first year, although I don't remember how. Then I made the best educational decision I ever made. I would stay in the same job in the same school (much to the principal's dismay), and I would succeed. Fortunately, I wasn't so stupid that I could not learn from what had happened. I had a great second year, and the rest of the time I spent at that school had its ups and downs but was generally quite wonderful.

These years as a grade seven teacher prepared me well for my present job, especially working with student teachers. Every mistake they make, I have made. Every problem they have, I have had. If I was going to survive as a teacher I knew that I had to figure out what was going on and how to use what I had going for me. I had to learn to teach in a real classroom of my own. And I did learn to teach.

I had three things going for me as a teacher then. First, I really liked kids—especially the daring, risking, try-anything attitude of junior high. Second, I worked very hard. Not that I wanted to compete; it's just that my father taught me that the world didn't owe me a living and I believed him. In addition, I liked to work. Third, I was creative. I could turn almost anything into a teaching activity. I watched what kids liked to do outside school, and I translated these into things I could use in my classes. Soon, I was replicating any television game show (or any other game) into a way to study and review the content of my subject area.

I struck on a simple but, for me, effective philosophy. Work from a philosophy of success instead of failure. You will see some of this philosophy described further in this book.

I still like teaching just as much as I did during my first years, even though my job has changed quite a bit. I continue to enjoy the "kids" that I meet. Except now these kids are much older. I still have the same abilities that I had when I started teaching, only hopefully they are more well developed. At the same time, I still don't have some things going for me that would make my life as a teacher much easier. I never was, nor am I now, organized. I have to work especially hard to keep on top of my organization. My office looks like an attic.

Today, my job as a teacher has changed. I read in my subject area, teach my undergraduate and graduate classes, work as a reading tutor at the elementary level and as a junior high youth sponsor in my church, coach baseball and basketball (my way to stay around junior high kids), try to create novel ways to do things, and write social studies textbooks for schools and books for university students. I still enjoy helping people achieve success and hope this book helps you as a teacher.

## LARRY

My childhood revolved around sports. By the age of eight my friends and I spent most of our time at the vacant lot alongside Richard Sobey's house or on the school grounds at St. Rita's. We played every sport in season—football in the fall, hockey in the winter, and baseball and softball in the spring and summer.

One fall my friends and I were fortunate enough to locate World War I surplus tank helmets selling for one dollar each. With these helmets, hockey shoulder pads, and our blue jeans carefully rolled inwards to just below the knees we were ready for full contact football. Jack Gorman's dad, a former intercollegiate football player, spent a morning demonstrating the intricacies of the offensive and defensive line stances for us. Following the practice we recruited additional players from the neighborhood and "scheduled" a game with a group from another neighborhood. No adults were involved. We scheduled the game, laid out rules, refereed using an honor system (called our own penalties) and proceeded to pound the "heck" out of each other. The first game took place on their turf and the next one on ours. This rotation continued for most of the fall. I soon found myself not only arranging the games but acting as a playing coach as we recruited new team members.

My newfound coaching status carried over into softball where I became playing coach of our playground softball team for four of the next five years. There was one season when we had an adult coach—

> **"Personal experience is all the experience we ever have."**
> *- Unknown*

Frankie Hopkins' dad, a great coach. It was a relief that season not to have to schedule practices, worry about who would not show up to games, lug bats, balls and bases over to the park on my bicycle, arrange for scorekeepers and umpires, and fill out line-up cards. A young boy should have other things to worry about.

The opening class of my first day of high school was physical education. I could not believe it! I was fascinated that such a course existed. I had never heard of physical education in elementary school. Of course, we played at recess, had a track and field day in the spring, and skated on an outdoor rink during the winter months but I had never had a scheduled physical education class.

I was very active in my high school's varsity sports programs. I ran cross-country and played basketball, hockey, and football. I mention my high school sports participation because it was my involvement with these teams and in particular the coaches that eventually solidified my interest in teaching as a career.

Father Jerome Killoran coached football and basketball. He was an excellent coach. Although he was an outstanding motivator and extremely knowledgeable in the technical skills of both sports, I remember him best for treating us as individuals and pushing each of us as far as our skills would allow. Even the least skilled player had a major team role to play. Father Killoran carried his coaching skills into the classroom where he taught Latin. I often wished I was as good at Latin as I was at sports. Although I persevered and Father Killoran provided all kinds of help, I still struggled. I passed each year but the effort was such that I chose not to study Latin in my last year of high school. A wise move on my part! Anyway, the point I want to make is that my Latin experience made me realize why Father Killoran was such a great coach and teacher. He cared! It was that simple. He expected all to put forth efforts commensurate with their abilities. If they didn't, he had a gentle but firm way of pushing until they did. He did not allow any of his students to sell themselves short.

Mr. Don Dufresne was a hockey and football coach who taught English. He too was an outstanding coach and teacher because he cared. In his coaching and teaching he paid little attention to natural ability and skill level; his major concern was that his charges were interested in learning and willing to work hard. You had the same feeling whether he was teaching you Shakespeare's *Merchant of Venice* or how to block a blitzing linebacker—he was just too nice a person to let down. As a result, everyone gave an honest effort. They wanted to do well because they wanted their efforts to reflect positively on Mr. Dufresne. He didn't overtly ask for this commitment; everyone gave it willingly. Although I had other excellent teachers, Mr. Dufresne and Father Killoran were by far the most influential and I think it was their modeling that most encouraged me to eventually enter teaching.

As the oldest of 10 children I didn't really think much about going to university as I was growing up. Times were simple. I had hopes for a professional hockey career and I had a good summer job painting barrels with a

> **"We should all be concerned about the future because that is where we will spend the remainder of our lives."**
> *Charles F. Kettering*

local oil dealership. If my hockey career did not materialize I knew I could always get full-time work from my summer employer. With hard work I could rise from barrel painter to truck driver in three or four years. My life was in order. But a hockey scholarship offer to Denver University changed it all. I quickly accepted the scholarship and I knew immediately what I wanted to study. I wanted to be a teacher. Upon arrival at D.U. a well-meaning counselor examined my high school transcripts and suggested that I consider a program in the Business Faculty since those graduates made much more money than teachers. The counselor was persuasive, but I held my ground and enrolled in the education program.

I majored in physical education and minored in mathematics. Upon graduation I took a physical education teaching job at a rural high school (approximately 800 students) in Blind River, Ontario. A few years later I moved to a nearby larger community, Sudbury, to a school with a population of close to 1700 students where I taught physical education and mathematics. Along with my teaching assignments I ran intramural programs and coached at least one major sport per season.

Although I was extremely busy, I enjoyed going to work every day. I enjoyed the young people I taught and coached. I learned much from them. On the whole, they were very receptive to and appreciative of everything I tried to do. I wasn't sure why I was getting a paycheck for something I was willing to do for nothing. All the reward I needed came from my students' faces. I had many successes. I also had what I considered to be a number of serious failures. There were some youngsters I just couldn't reach and others I didn't care to reach. I still feel bad about this, even today, more than 25 years after the fact.

It amazes me that I can pick up old yearbooks from my high school teaching days and still remember so many of the children by name, and give a very rich description of each child's interests, abilities, likes and dislikes, and even name a number of his or her school friends. They obviously made an indelible mark upon my soul. I am richer for having known them. I am richer for having chosen teaching as a career. I still enjoy teaching. This isn't surprising since it still involves people. My students are older and more experienced now and I continue to learn much from them.

## A FINAL WORD

"Why do you teach?" This is a question we have each heard many times. We have been asked this by young students in both elementary and secondary schools. By undergraduate students considering teaching as a career. By practicing teachers who, we suspect, are questioning themselves in a circuitous way. The motive for the question often seems to be the same. Why would a rational adult intentionally seek the presence of sometimes engaging, often rambunctious, sometimes mind-stretching, and sometimes ego-shattering children and adolescents?

Good questions have many answers. "Why do you teach?" is a good question. We hope you will be stimulated to search for your own answer.

## READINGS FOR EXTENSION AND ENRICHMENT

Lipka, Richard P, Ed. Brinthaupt, Thomas M, Ed. (1999). *The Role of Self in Teacher Development.* Albany, New York: State University of New York Press. Addresses the importance of balancing the personal development of teachers with their professional development.

Norlander-Case, Kay A. Reagan, Timothy G. Case, Charles W. (1999). *The Professional Teacher: The Preparation and Nurturance of the Reflective Practitioner.* San Francisco, California: Jossey-Bass Inc. Offers a comprehensive account of what goes into the substance and process of preparing professional educators, from selection to induction into teaching.

Parsons, Jim & Beauchamp, Larry. (1991). *Stories of teaching.* Richmond Hill, ON: Scholastic Canada Ltd. A collection of vignettes that provides an honest, supportive look at teaching as a grand human vocation.

Phillips, Marian B., Hatch, J Amos (1999). *Why Teach? Prospective Teachers' Reasons for Entering the Profession.* Paper presented at the Reconceptualizing Early Childhood Education Conference, Columbus, OH. Details an analysis of prospective early childhood teachers' responses on a university application to the question "Why are you interested in becoming a teacher?"

Serow, Robert C. (1993). Why Teach?: Altruism and Career Choice among Nontraditional Recruits to Teaching. *Journal of Research & Development in Education, 26* (4), 197-20. Views teaching principally as a means of enhancing self-efficacy or other aspects of personal satisfaction.

# CHAPTER 2

# Understanding the Need to Achieve

*YOU cannot put the same shoe on every foot.*

**- PUBLILIUS SYRUS**

## INTRODUCTION

Teaching is about helping students achieve. Yet, how many times have you heard this statement? "Teaching would be easy if it weren't for the students." The statement sounds cynical, but it rings true for most, if not all, teachers. Why do students complicate the formula of schools by making teaching difficult?

On one level, the answer to this question is relatively easy. Students are people, and like all people they have needs. If there's one thing particularly true about students it is that they are not hesitant to express their needs. Sometimes, in fact often, they express their needs in ways that frustrate the plans of teachers.

While it is not possible to address every need that students may have, there are some general needs that almost all students have. What are these students' needs, and how can a teacher even begin to address them? Just listing needs is not quite enough for the thoughtful teacher.

There are also a number of important questions about student needs that teachers must answer. For example, what should the balance be between concern for student needs and concern for the curriculum? If a teacher worries too much about student needs, can this concern get in the way of teaching? Are there times when it is unwise to try to address student needs at all?

## WHAT ARE YOUR STUDENTS' NEEDS?

Let's start with a discussion of students' needs. If you are in a university class, you might be laughing to yourself. University professors talking about students' needs? What a joke. If your experience is typical, you may believe that there is no group better than university professors for ignoring students' needs or for acting like students' needs were the least worthwhile of all educational priorities.

In a short article [Dear professor: This is what I want you to know. 68(6), 1986] in *Phi Delta Kappan*, Workman tells about a high school class that was asked to write a letter to a professor outlining some of the things professors should know about them. In the article, these students identified four needs that they especially wanted their professors to know about: (1) a search for family, (2) identity problems and loneliness, (3) living with rapid change, and (4) fear of failure.

It is this fourth need, the fear of failure that we will explore throughout the remainder of this chapter. However, rather than discussing the fear of failure, let's restate it in a more positive light and structure the ensuing discussion around the need to achieve. This seems logical since much of teaching is about helping kids to achieve.

## THE NEED TO ACHIEVE

All students in our schools need to experience success. But the fact is that many students do not succeed. Why not? Why can't all students succeed?

First, given the way that our educational system has developed, some students are not academically capable enough to succeed. These students either lack the "ability" (a curious term often used by professional educators), or have abilities that do not match the criteria set out for them by the curriculum (both explicit and hidden) that they will face. In some schools, these students are ironically called "special." The truth is that schools offer these students little chance of personal success and, because schools are the nesting place for society, they stand little chance of success later in life.

Some students don't even try to achieve. At first glance, their lack of willingness to try is surprising because, from a practical sense, if a student doesn't achieve at a satisfactory level, that student won't pass on to the next grade. Some students—a few—just don't care about anything. And, no matter what a teacher does, these students can't be made to care.

Some students care about the wrong things. Recent research on peer group importance in student lives suggests that most students are motivated by the need to belong. For some, the object of their belonging is for shorter terms than the kind of rewarded belonging school offers. It's not that these students actively choose not to get good grades; it's more that they choose to fulfill their needs for acceptance and belonging in other areas of their lives. Often, the reason these students don't get good grades is that achievement to them means something other than getting a good grade. They choose to achieve outside rather than inside school.

Then there are "regular" kids. Most teachers call them the "good" kids. When asked, they may state that they hate school. However, they won't actively express this hate in ways that will disrupt their teachers' classrooms. They simply don't need the grief.

These are the kids who seem to care about almost everything. School is just like all the other areas of their lives. Without much thinking about it, they survive from day to day as well as they can. They don't have specific plans for the long-range future. They aren't particularly alienated. They're just kids. They persevere.

> **"Children need love, especially when they do not deserve it."**
> *- Harold Hulbert*

School, for these "good" kids, is just one more thing to do and one more chance for them to follow the directions of those who are above them. They just don't seem to mind having people be above them. Much has been written recently about self-esteem. "Good" kids are the ones who get just enough self-esteem from the activities of school that they go on doing school, without ever worrying about rebelling. It's not that they don't care; it's more that they never thought that it was crucial to care too much.

Then there are kids who thrive on school. School is their niche. They are the lucky ones (or are they?) for whom the rules of school match almost perfectly the rules of their lives. Some have plans. They knew what they wanted to be when they were three or four years old—things like corporate lawyers. Seriously, some students begin consciously considering life after school even before they go to school. By the time they are seven, they know what they want to be and they believe that the things they are learning in grade two can help them reach their goals.

For the latter two groups, teachers have little to do to help them achieve. Just lay out the goods and watch these students go after them. Sure, some will take the bait faster than others, but they will all be motivated. If there were only these sorts of children in schools, the life of a teacher would be much easier.

Gray hairs in teachers are caused by the first two groups of children. Teachers keep asking us, "How can these students be motivated to achieve?" The answer is that they are already motivated to achieve. They need to achieve. The problem is that while the needs of the last two groups are being met in schools, the needs of the first two groups have no chance of being met by the typical activities of school. They want to achieve, but too often they want to achieve at the wrong things.

Knowing what you do about these two "troublesome" groups, you have two choices as a teacher. The choice made by most teachers is not to care about the first two groups, or to quit caring if it gets to be too much work. Most teachers who quit caring will continue to be pleasant, cordial, and as fair as possible to these students; but the curriculum is the curriculum, and there just isn't enough time or energy to actively do anything to help students who seem to actively fight anything you do. If you listen to teachers talk, you will be able to spot those who have made this choice. They often start things by saying: "There isn't enough time in the day to ..." or "We don't get paid enough to ..." or "If I ... I would have to neglect the majority of the class."

> "Some things have to be believed to be seen."
> - *Ralph Hodgson*

We understand what these teachers are saying. While we think they are wrong-minded to make this choice, we don't blame them one bit. There is logic in the choice, and they have chosen this logical alternative—probably they see it as their only way to survive. But remember, we are two teachers with our heads in the clouds who have said things like, "There isn't enough idealism in the world." We think that teachers should not give up on kids. We also think that there are some real rewards for both teachers and students in purposely setting out to help all students achieve.

First, there is a reward in knowing that you are trying to help another human being. We know from our own experience how important one person's influence can be on another person. Even one teacher who tries to help another person can make a huge difference in that person's life. In some cases that teacher can forever alter the life of a person he or she has helped. Reason #1: If you work at it, you can actually help another person.

Second, you are doing your job. We believe in work. We believe in teaching as a job—a vocation. We don't believe that the only reason to work is to make money. For us there is a special reward for being able to say to yourself that you are doing your job well—you are being a teacher in the best sense of the word. Teachers, as far as we know, don't take a Hippocratic Oath; but they should. The job of a teacher means that you help all the students in your class. Reason #2: You help people because it's your job.

Third, we trust the research of Abraham Maslow. Maslow studied the motivation for humans to act. He theorized that there was a pattern in the reasons humans were inspired to work. He identified high level and a low level motivators. From highest to lowest, here are Maslow's levels of motivation to act: (1) to serve, (2) to achieve, (3) to belong, (4) to be secure, and (5) to survive. Reason #3: We believe that the highest level of human motivation is "to serve."

The first need of students is the need to achieve. Fortunately, achievement is the focus of the school. Achievement is not only what passes a student from one grade to the next; it is what motivates students to be passed. What a wonderful match! If you want to help children learn how to achieve, there is simply no better place to do this than the school.

The question for other chapters and other books is how, specifically, a teacher can help students learn to achieve. But, for now, the point is to name achievement as a necessary need for students, a necessary focus for teachers, and a perfect fit for schools. Still, there is the haunting problem: if you want to help meet all the students' needs for achievement, you have to offer your classes more than the typical activities of school.

## REASONS FOR LOW ACHIEVEMENT

If you ever listen to the old Broadway musical *West Side Story*, you will hear a tongue-in-cheek song where the gangs on New York's West side are telling a cop that they get in trouble with the law because their home life is all messed up and they are basically just misunderstood. Certainly, they couldn't be any part of the problem. Finally, after listening to all the excuses, the song ends by stating that the gang members didn't need a psychiatrist but a "year in the pen." As Officer Krupkee puts it in one line of the song, "It ain't just a question of misunderstood, deep down inside he's just no good!"

We tend to agree with the spirit of this song. Even though there may be logical reasons for student behaviors, we also believe that students must be held responsible for what they do. So far, we have discussed the student as a reason for low achievement. But we have never suggested, and we never will, that teachers should excuse the lack of student achievement. One of the most important jobs teachers have is to highlight and stress standards and goals to which their students must aspire. Without such educational goals, education will all but stop.

However, there are a number of reasons for low achievement that have little to do with the student. If teachers do not know or understand these reasons, they will have a difficult time shaping the environment of their classrooms. Here are some possible explanations for a lack of achievement that lie outside the student:

**Reason One:** The lack of student success may be teacher related. For example, a teacher's background and culture and a student's background and culture may differ. Teachers with middle-class backgrounds may have some difficulty understanding and motivating working-class and lower-class students. Why? Because they haven't lived the culture and don't understand it.

**Reason Two:** Teachers see students as inadequate. One hundred years ago, when teachers looked out at their classrooms, they saw a group of empty vessels (students) that needed filling. Illiteracy was equated with crime. What did teachers do? They did the only thing they could. They filled their students with content, and they did it as efficiently as possible. Students were seen as inadequate, and as having a deficit that needed to be remedied. Students' rights or personalities were not important. In fact, they got in the way.

Much has changed today. When teachers look out over their classrooms, they see young people capable of doing or learning what young people that age can do or learn. Why has the view of most teachers changed? First, the field of educational psychology has outlined the stages through which young people grow. It has also suggested methodologies of teaching that "work best" at different stages. Second, individual rights have become important to educators. Students can no longer be treated the same because they are no longer seen as the same. Even if they were, most students would not stand for it.

Still, some teachers look out over their classrooms and see problems waiting to happen. Some teachers see the world as a series of gunfights that they must win or die. Some see every action as a threat to their peaceful kingdom. Some even see their students as stupid, either unable or unwilling to learn.

But young people are not stupid. They look back at their teachers and most know exactly what the teacher is thinking. Still, they are young and they respect what their teachers say and think—even if it is ignorant or even if it is about them. Students react to the perceptions of their teachers. This is called the self-fulfilling prophecy. Why do many students fail to achieve? Because their teachers tell them in words, looks, or deeds that they cannot achieve. And, unfortunately, their students believe them.

> **"Two men look out through the same bars: One sees the mud, and one the stars."**
> *- Frederick Langbridge*

**Reason Three:** Some students fail to achieve because they are not encouraged to achieve. Students will do just what their teachers expect them to do. If a teacher has low standards of performance, these low standards encourage students not to perform. If teachers come from different backgrounds than students and if teachers perceive their students as inadequate, then low performance often becomes acceptable to both students and teachers.

Teachers can add to the problem already existing by expecting little. They may also, in good conscience, praise students for less than satisfactory work. This praise has a certain logic to it. Teachers want to encourage self-esteem and do not want to foster hopelessness. But lasting self-esteem only comes when real work, challenging work is carried out successfully. The effects of low standards can be numbing. Students may not be encouraged to work hard.

**Reason Four:** Sometimes students fail to achieve because they are not grouped with other students who can help them achieve. This statement is not a commercial for homogeneous grouping. In fact, homogeneous grouping can encourage mediocrity. Ineffective groups of students may include those who are socially, academically, or physically incompatible. The plain truth is that some kids just don't work well together, for whatever reasons. If you are a teacher, know that ineffective groupings can exist. Watch for them, and if you see them, change them.

**Reason Five:** Some students fail to learn because teaching conditions are poor. If the teaching-learning environment is uncomfortable, students may fall even further behind academically. When teaching conditions are poor, both teachers and students experience frustration and discouragement, behavior problems increase, and it is difficult to provide a productive learning environment. We have taught the same university class to a similar number of students in two different classrooms in the same term. One classroom was large and roomy; the other was small and cramped. Even though the class format did not change from day to day in the two classes, few people in the large, roomy classroom missed class. But in the small classroom, attendance was not as regular. As a result of not attending, the grades were poorer.

## NON-TEACHER REASONS FOR LACK OF ACHIEVEMENT

There are also some non-teacher related causes for lack of achievement. Some of these include the differences between school and parental norms. Sometimes no matter how hard teachers work, students just don't achieve because they are not taught to care to achieve.

Remember, not even the greatest teaching ideas will work if students don't care. Caring, on the part of the student, is a given. If students don't care to achieve, or don't care to work, or don't care about the rewards that are "promised" as part of the natural order of the reward system of the school, no amount of struggle, work, sweat, or even prayer will help. But if students care or can be taught to care, the world can be opened up.

So, if caring is important for student achievement, why don't students care? One reason is that they have cared once upon a time, but have been taught that caring is a wasted effort. We think one of the greatest current sins of modern school systems is that student effort is not rewarded. Some schools, in the name of standards, norm or curve grades so that no matter how hard some kids work they fall at the low end of the curve. Our university students have complained of this.

> **"The meaning of things lies not in the things themselves but in our attitude towards them."**
> *- Antoine de Saint-Exupery*

Recently students in one of our university classes, almost in one voice, said that no matter how hard they worked in classes where a normal curve was used to grade student papers and exams, they all got middle-of-the-road grades. The result: the class, without much being said out loud, quit working so hard. Interestingly, they believed that they got the same grades as they would have if they had killed themselves with work. They had learned something about the use of the normal curve—it will adjust itself to the personality and the will of the class. A lazy, hard-to-motivate class can shape the curve in the same way that a motivated, hard-working class can shape the curve. What did they learn? That their achievement in terms of grades did not rest in their own hands or on the sweat of their own brows. Instead, it rested on a system that could be manipulated. So, what did they do? They manipulated the system.

Our students were clever, but in the long run self-defeating. We would rather have had them working hard and learning as much as possible. These are education students who should be, theoretically, working for more noble goals, like the love of learning. But they were like everyone else. They were motivated by grades. More true to the story they told us, they were dis-motivated by grades.

No matter how energetically some students begin their work as students, the lack of previous success will eventually pull them back like a great magnet. Most of us cannot keep caring when caring is repeatedly shown to be fruitless. The real heroes in schools are those students who, because of a lack of natural intelligence, have a history that is defined by their lack of success. Still, some of these kids retain a pleasant disposition and personality in spite of their constant losing. More astonishing to us than almost anything, they keep on trying—even if they have not succeeded in the past. These kids are the real salt of the earth. They are the kids we want to marry our sons and daughters. They are simply good people!

Sometimes, the presence of negative peer pressure can stop students from succeeding. Peer pressure works in an interesting way. Research studies about peer groups suggest that these groups hardly ever vocally encourage kids to do bad things. But kids' needs to be accepted are so strong (they fear rejection) that they try to guess what will play with the peer group and live up, or rather down, to that level.

Another problem that keeps students from achieving is inappropriate curriculum and instruction. A classroom is a marvelous mirror of society. Our experience is that in any class, regardless of grade level, there will be about twenty average kids (don't read this as meaning that all the kids are the same), about two kids smarter than the teacher will ever hope to be, and about five kids who can't read. They're not bad kids, or even stupid kids; they just can't read. When this mish-mash of students is given homogeneous lesson plans, at least some of them won't have a clue. The impact of reading ability plays a tremendous part in what you can do as a teacher in your classroom. And, don't forget, reading level is just one of a whole range of possible differences.

Many administrators would use this "student differences" idea to call for homogeneous classrooms—ability grouping. We wouldn't. For one thing, attempts to "homogenize" students are prone to failure because it just can't be done. The differences are simply too great. Furthermore, we like the differences. Don't mistake our note above as a complaint that kids come to class with differences. We just want you to know that not all your kids will be the same. The tendency is to see differences as a problem, but they might just as easily be seen as variety—golden opportunities for creative teaching.

## A FINAL WORD

Over the years, the things we have learned to appreciate most about the kids in our classes are not those things that have made teaching easier. Instead, we have grown to like those things that have made teaching more interesting. We never went into teaching because it was easy and we haven't been disappointed on this count.

## READINGS FOR EXTENSION AND ENRICHMENT

Bhattacharyya, Maitrayee (1998). Creating a New Research Agenda on Race, Gender, and Class Impacts on Educational Achievement and Underachievement. *A Workshop on Race, Gender, Class, and Student Achievement.* Washington, D.C.: National Educational Research Policy and Priorities Board. Presents the results of a workshop on race, gender, class, and student achievement

DuFour, Richard, Eaker, Robert (1998). *Professional Learning Communities at Work: Best Practices for Enhancing Student Achievement.* Bloomington, IN: National Education Service. This book offers recommendations for those who seek to transform their school into a professional learning community as characterized by an environment fostering mutual cooperation, emotional support, personal growth, and a synergy of efforts

Lee, Patrick W. (1999). In Their Own Voices: An Ethnographic Study of Low-Achieving Students within the Context of School Reform. *Urban Education, 34* (2), 214-44. Investigates the causes of school failure from a student perspective through interviews with 40 urban high school students experiencing academic difficulties.

Lumsden, Linda (1997). *Expectations for Students.* ERIC Digest, Number 116 (Report No. EDO-EA-97-8). Washington, DC: Office of Educational Research and Improvement. (ERIC Document Reproduction Service No. ED409609). This digest synthesizes recent research about teachers' expectations and the ways in which teachers' expectations affect student performance.

Reavis, Charles A., Vinson, David, Fox, Richard (1999). Importing a Culture of Success Via a Strong Principal. *Clearing House, 72* (4), 199-202. Describes how a high school principal emphasized achievement at the highest levels through heroes and heroines, rites and rituals, stories, governance and leadership, symbols, enforcing expectations, and serving as the "high priest" of the high-achievement culture.

Tauber, Robert T. (1998). *Good or Bad, What Teachers Expect from Students They Generally Get!* ERIC Digest (Report No. EDO-SP-97-7). District of Columbia, U.S.A. (ERIC Document Reproduction Service No. ED426985). Discusses the Pygmalion effect, or the idea that one's expectations about a person can eventually lead that person to behave and achieve in ways that conform to those expectations.

# CHAPTER 3

# nteracting

*"If A doctor, lawyer, or dentist had 40 people in his office at one time, all of whom had different needs, and some of whom didn't want to be there and were causing trouble, and the doctor, lawyer, or dentist, without assistance, had to treat them all with professional excellence for nine months, then he might have some conception of the classroom teacher's job."*

**-DONALD D. QUINN**

## INTRODUCTION

It is important to remember that teachers are people. It is also important to remember that people differ from one another. These differences are a good thing. In teaching, too, differences are positive. Why, then, do we seem to have an idea that teachers should be clones of each other?

Often books and courses in teacher education implicitly suggest that all teachers are the same. Courses may teach one style of lesson planning to the exclusion of others. Courses encourage similar teacher classroom behaviors, just as if all teachers had the same skills and personalities. But you know that this is not true. All teachers are not created the same.

Whenever books or university courses direct readers or students to a similarity of behavior, they are implicitly suggesting that teachers all act the same. Or, if teachers are not acting the same, that they should be. But good teachers differ. When we ask our university students to recall their good teachers and to share what made them so good, it is surprising how their reactions to these good teachers differ. Some are remembered for their ability to lecture. They "knew their stuff." Some because they "cared" and "treated their students like individuals." Some because, for one reason or another, they "made a difference" in the lives of students.

Teachers differ in experience, wisdom, subject matter, gender, age, marital status, social background, cultural background, ability, interests, temperament, and philosophy. Often there is a range of similarity. Elementary teachers often say that they "teach children and not subject matter." High school teachers tend to think of themselves as "subject area specialists." But these general ways of thinking are not cut and dried. Even within subject area specialists, there can be a wide range of behavior differences.

It's not just a difference between good and bad teachers. We would hesitate to suggest that cynical teachers are good. We would also suggest that abusive teachers can never be tolerated. But some good teachers use humor; some don't. Some good teachers talk a lot in the classroom; some seldom talk. Some are gregarious; others are simply shy. The point of suggesting that the behavior patterns of good teachers can vary widely is to suggest that, regardless of what personality type you are, if you work hard and have some basic personal tools, you can probably find a way of teaching that you can use effectively and that will enhance your personality. This is a positive statement. We are saying right now that, if you commit yourself to the task, you can become a good teacher!

Teachers are not the only part of the educational equation where there are differences. The schools where teachers work vary just as dramatically as the teachers who work in them. Furthermore, the students that teachers teach vary even more widely than the teachers.

Here's a bit of advice: be leery of those who talk about or imply the need for cultural uniformity among teachers. Our experience suggests that their goals and interests are more in line with bureaucratic or industrial efficiency than they are with education. They want to administrate, not teach.

## INTERACTING WITH STUDENTS

Can you imagine a time when teachers didn't believe that they should talk to or have interactions with students? The idea that teachers work without encouraging the interactions of their students seems foreign to us today. But less than 150 years ago, teachers had a much different idea of what students were like and how they should be treated.

Until the late 1800's, educational systems and teachers believed that the teacher's goal should be to impart content knowledge to a passive student—to fill an empty vessel. Teaching methodologies consisted mostly of lecture, questioning students on catechism (either secular or sacred), and giving students oral or written exams. The power always rested with the teacher. The power never was given to the students. It wasn't a case of being nasty. It was just that, frankly, it didn't matter what the student thought or considered. The student's job was simple. He or she came to the exchange with a deficit that needed filling. The teacher had the stuff to do the filling. The question was simply what to fill, how much to fill, and how quickly students could be filled. The student's job was to take in the content given by the teacher, learn it with as much fidelity as possible, and give it back to the teacher when the teacher called for it.

If you read and consider histories of educational thought, you will discover the reasons why this teaching methodology was considered appropriate, and even necessary. Quite simply, there were two reasons for such methodologies. First, in the past people had a different idea of authority. In part, authority was based on educational status. In the mid-1800's, there were few educated people in many communities. Those who were educated held a high status. They were listened to and respected. Today, of course, a larger portion of society can read and write. Educational attainment is no longer an aberration, but the norm.

A second reason was that 150 years ago society was going through an industrial revolution. The changes made in society were tremendously fast-paced and radical. Families and traditional values were uprooted and altered. Educators and others were concerned about what was happening to people. They looked out over society, saw the difficulties, and were worried. As always, these people saw one institution most capable of re-establishing control to the out-of-control society—the schools.

Whenever and however they could, these educators built control into the educational system in terms of interaction patterns. The best way to keep control was to put the teacher and the school in

> **"We have met the enemy, and it is us."**
> - Pogo

charge of it. To give just one example of how this educational thinking worked in terms of restructuring methodology, educators looked at society and asked: "It's out of control; how can we control it? Let's make a curriculum that exerts control; what will it be?" One answer: there is nothing more controlled and ordered than spelling. Spelling was the content area that had the greatest control inherent in it; so, in an attempt to order and control, the schools built a whole curriculum around spelling.

Times have changed. Although it is sometimes easy to find teachers who act as if they should control every aspect of the classroom, it would be almost impossible to find a teacher who says he or she believes that students should have no say in their curriculum or classroom activities. When did this change? The answer is that the change has been recent, very recent.

Just sixty years ago, educators were still extolling traditional thinking. Waller's book *The Sociology of Teaching* (Waller, W., 1932, New York: Russell & Russell) was a classic work that addressed teacher-student relationships. Waller believed that the teacher was an authority figure in classrooms. In fact, the largest part of the teacher's job was to be that authority figure.

Waller' s reasons were simple. He believed that teachers had to maintain their authority or they would run into trouble. They had to establish distance from their students to maintain discipline. And last, they had to demonstrate to those outside classrooms that their students respected them. Students should show their teachers admiration. How well did teachers learn these traditional beliefs? Quite well, thank you. Research shows that student teachers still see student control as a primary focus in teaching.

But recent research contradicts the belief in the idea of the distant teacher. Instead, the research suggests that if teachers are to increase their students' achievement, they should act quite differently. Rather than remaining distant, teachers must form personal bonds with students if they are to teach them. Some of the research says that it works. The best way to explain it is to say simply that affection is a stronger motivator than admiration. Second, students and their parents now expect that teachers will have a different relationship with them. While we see many advantages with the new interacting roles of students and teachers, these new patterns of distance and closeness create an ambiguity in the teacher's role. For you, there are some practical questions: what role will you take within your classroom and with your students and teachers? What kind of culture do you want in your classroom? These are not unimportant questions; nor are they simple to answer. If you are like most beginning teachers, you will spend quite a bit of time answering them.

## INTERACTING WITH OTHER TEACHERS

How enjoyable it could be if people would work together. But, alas, they do not. One of the themes of this book is that, at present, teaching is one of the loneliest jobs in the world. Teachers teach in the same place, but they seldom teach together. We keep telling you this because we hope that it is possible to change that aspect. We would like to think that our work moves the profession of teaching toward a more cooperative and complementary understanding of itself.

Our working together on this book is a testimony to how teachers can support each other. Both of us have very different skills, talents, and personalities. We are friends and we like each other, but in our partnership we each do different things. To be brief, it works for us. We think that teachers should try working together, coming to a situation where they are able to magnify their strengths and help each other overcome their weaknesses.

It has been said: "Teachers have peers but not colleagues." Doesn't that strike you as odd? Is there any other job where there are so many people around? Yet, teachers typically work in isolation. Why? Frankly, we don't know. Maybe teachers fear that other people will see the mistakes they make. It certainly isn't that teachers like to do all the work by themselves.

We do know some things about teachers. Teachers have described the ideal colleague as helpful, but not pushy. Teachers are hesitant to ask for help in areas of serious difficulty. Asking for help might be perceived as a weakness. Teachers also hesitate to tell a peer to do something different. But, we say, four eyes are better than two—especially if they are looking at what is happening from different perspectives. What kind of a friend would see something he or she could help fix and not lend a hand?

One of the problems is school itself. The norms of schools are fixed to the point that they do not support a culture of observing others teach, making suggestions for improvement, and discussing professional problems. Too often, teachers never do find another person with whom they dare talk about their own teaching difficulties. Too bad, because it's hard to improve all by yourself.

A good critical friend—one who cares about you, and one who dares tell you what he or she thinks without a risk to the friendship—is hard to find. It's easy enough to find a

> **"A new idea is delicate. It can be killed by a sneer or yawn; it can be stabbed to death by a quip and worried to death by a frown on the right man's brow."**
> *- Charles Brower*

person who will mush you to death with false praise. It's also easy to find a person who will be critical. But, a critical friend? That's a hard one. Why are we telling you this? Because we want you to know that it is possible, and especially desirable, to find one. If you do, you will survive more easily as a teacher.

## INTERACTING WITH ADMINISTRATORS

Interactions with students are one thing. Interactions with colleagues are another. But how should teachers treat and be treated by principals? This question, because of the amount of power involved between the teacher and the principal, is more difficult and more risky.

Often teachers put themselves in an ambiguous position. They want to have their cake and eat it too. They want principals to leave them alone, not to interfere with their daily classrooms. On the other hand, they want administrators to serve as buffers to outside pressures such as parents, board administrators, and the community. They want to run their own classrooms, but want principals to help enforce student discipline. They want principals to back them in their discipline policies and develop and maintain school discipline policies.

## INTERACTING WITH PARENTS

Interactions with parents can also be difficult. The only thing that, unfortunately, makes interactions with parents easier is that teachers typically have few interactions with them. When a teacher sees a parent, often it is in times of crisis and when a student is either in academic difficulty or is in behavioral difficulty. On the other hand, when students progress reasonably, teachers may only see parents at twice yearly conferences, if then.

This is hardly the ideal relationship. A better relationship would be for parents to support the teacher and teachers to support the parents. Instead, teachers often want parents to attend to their requests, without interfering with their teaching plans.

## INTERACTING WITH CURRICULUM

Teachers interact with curriculum at a number of levels in any given classroom. The explicit curriculum, by this we mean the "official party line," is familiar to all teachers. There are two types of explicit curriculum—curriculum-as-plan and curriculum-in-use. Curriculum-as-plan usually includes teacher developed long-term and short-term plans and government curriculum documents. Teachers often modify written plans—both those designed by the authorities and those designed by themselves—when they introduce them into their classrooms. The reasons for doing this are many. The material to be taught is too easy or too difficult. You have less or more time available than you had hoped for. The students are more interested or less interested than you thought they might be. The reasons for teacher modification of written plans could go on. But we are sure you get the point—the curriculum-in-use often differs from the curriculum-as-plan. These differences are introduced by individual teachers depending upon the context of each class they are teaching.

So far we have talked about how teachers interact with the explicit curriculum. There are at least two other curriculums operating in every classroom that are worthy of teacher attention. In every class and in every school, a hidden curriculum works to structure the actions of both teachers and students. But neither teachers nor students are specifically aware of when the hidden curriculum works. For example, student and teacher reality is structured by and yet supportive of a large institutionalized and socialized environment. Having one's life structured by bells in predetermined time blocks, and being bombarded daily by separate and discrete facts to learn and teach places students and teachers alike within a structure that is so self-evident and non-reflective that no one even considers it. And because no one thinks about it, its impact is hidden.

Another curriculum that is common to every classroom is the null curriculum. The null curriculum comprises everything the teacher leaves out or ignores when selecting what students ought to learn or experience. Analyzing the null curriculum forces teachers to question why "A" is included in the program and not "B." Individual teachers must consider a wide range of possibilities and then choose deliberately what they think students ought to learn.

## A FINAL WORD

The people interactions of teaching are complex. Teachers come to know students, administrators, and parents as people. This can be a problem. When you know people, it's hard not to feel responsible for them. Teaching would be much easier if students, administrators and parents didn't have personalities. But they do! Most people are not combative. They're just regular folks, wonderfully confusing and demanding.

Subject matter interactions can become confusing. After you have taught for a few years, what you originally thought was the subject matter no longer seems like the real subject matter. It's usually at this point some student has the audacity to ask, "Why do we have to study this?" This is often a tough question because we, as teachers, have never seriously asked this of ourselves.

In addition to becoming confusing, subject matter seems to grow as we teach. It becomes a curious mixture of what the authorized curriculum says is important, what you, the teachers, think should be stressed and what you believe your students need to know at any given time. These interactions result in subject matter that is less defined and more intuitive.

## READINGS FOR EXTENSION AND ENRICHMENT

Banks, Carmelita B. (1991). Harmonizing Student-Teacher Interactions: A Case for Learning Styles. *Synthesis, 2* (2), 1-5. Examines ways that teachers, students, parents, and administrators can work together for optimal learning.

Burke, Kay, Ed. (1995). *Managing the Interactive Classroom: A Collection of Articles.* Palatine, Illinois: IRI/Skylight Training and Publishing, Inc. Intended for teachers, this book is a compilation of articles on effectively creating and maintaining an interactive classroom, one in which the teacher uses a wide repertoire of teaching strategies, organizational tools, problem-solving techniques, and consensus building methods.

Doyle, W. (1990). Classroom Knowledge as a Foundation for Teaching. *Teachers College Record, 3*, 348-360. A useful framework for creating teaching practices grounded in the realities of school settings.

Johnston, Betty (1995). Fostering Meaningful Teacher Interactions among Primary and Junior Teachers through Collegial Efforts (Ed.D. Practicum Report, Nova Southeastern University). Describes a practicum project that sought to improve professional communication among staff at an urban, public elementary school where teachers did not have opportunities to meaningfully interact with one another.

Meichtry, Yvonne J. (1990). *Teacher Collaboration: The Effects of Interdisciplinary Teaming on Teacher Interactions and Classroom Practices.* Paper presented at the Annual Meeting of the Mid-Western Educational Research Association, Chicago, Illinois. Explores an aspect of school organization that has the potential to influence teacher interactions and the classroom practices of teachers.

# CHAPTER 4

# Establishing Authority and Legitimacy

*THE weaker the man in authority. . .the stronger his insistence that all his privileges be acknowledged.*

**-AUSTIN O'MALLEY**

## INTRODUCTION

During Ronald Reagan's presidency, a report entitled *Chaos in the Classroom: Enemy of American Education* was issued by the Working Group on School Violence and Discipline. The report was issued from Reagan's Cabinet Council on Human Resources. The unsigned report is usually credited to Gary Bauer, Deputy Undersecretary of Education, and has become known as The Bauer Report. The Bauer Report studied school discipline and management problems and recommended a series of actions.

The Report stated that schools were in "chaos." The Report was not shy about where to put the blame for the turmoil. School discipline problems began when students gained the legal protection of due process against arbitrary actions by school officials. The Report asserted that the extension of constitutional rights to students has tied the hands of school administrators in their dealings with troublemakers.

After the problems were identified, the Report then postured a few models for dealing with classroom discipline. One model Reagan recommended as a "good" disciplinarian was Joseph Clark, a New Jersey principal. Clark personally had responded to his school's discipline problems by expelling 10% of his students during his first week on the job. Later, he cleaned up the school by getting rid of more than one-half of the school's student population—those who were the "real troublemakers."

With the help of Reagan's praise and the attention of a worshipful media, Clark became a sort of folk hero—an educational Clint Eastwood who rode in and cleaned up the town. Clark's strict approach to discipline eventually resulted in a 50% dropout or "pushout" rate. But such a rate is justified, Clark says. He credits his techniques with improving the minimum competency test scores of his 3000 students in just six months.

What do you think of Clark's actions? Scary, or a justifiable reaction to a difficult situation? Are Clark's actions the stuff of hero movies or horror flicks? Do they strike as resonant a chord with you as they did with many in the North American public?

We won't hide our feelings. At best, we think people like Clark are short-sighted. At worst, we find them arrogant, presumptuous, and dictatorial. If Clark's actions strike you as justifiable, let us ask you a couple of pertinent questions. Should students be systematically denied constitutional and human rights? What do the students who stay in school learn about dealing with other humans? What do the students who get tossed out learn? What happens to the 50% of his students who are pushed out into a community and a society with high youth unemployment? Do you personally think that about 50% of students are "losers"? Or is it 20% or 40%, or maybe even 80%? Would you be willing to flush out 50% of the students for the sake of the other 50%? What are the social costs to the fabric of North American society? And, if the phrase "social costs to the fabric of society" strikes you as a bit too "airy-fairy" liberal, what are the economic costs of trying to support a 50% failure rate of students caused by dumping uneducated, unskilled, unmotivated, and un-successful young people onto an already glutted labor market?

## WHY DO WE THINK CLARK MADE A MISTAKE?

Clark is probably a sincere educator who believes that when he punishes discipline offenders (half of the school's population), he is sacrificing the few to save the many—the 50% of the students who really care. But it strikes us that Clark is sweeping at least half his problems under the carpet. There is no doubt that he has solved his immediate problem of classroom management. He also seems to solve an immediate problem of low academic achievement by posturing higher test scores. But does he really?

Surely, the improvement of his students on minimum competency tests is accurate. In fact, we would expect an embarrassingly high improvement. Why? Because he has dumped students who have had a history of not being successful. When he kept them from taking the tests, he eliminated the students who were most likely to pull the school's average down. The only students who took the tests are the ones who have been successful. Without teaching a lick, any teacher or principal can improve the class average by dumping students who would tend to bring the class average down.

But most distressing to us is that Clark and those like him never seem to ask themselves some really important questions about discipline and class management. Why do students misbehave? Why don't some students care? Is there a relationship between lack of success and misbehavior? And, the central question to this chapter, what can teachers do to promote the kinds of classrooms where their students can succeed and where they will not be out of control?

## WHAT IS THE DIFFERENCE BETWEEN PUNISHMENT AND DISCIPLINE?

We have called this chapter "Establishing Authority and Legitimacy" instead of "How to Discipline Your Class," "How to Control Students," "How to Make Students Sit Down and Shut Up," or even "Discipline and Management" because we want to make an important point about discipline and management right at the start. Classroom discipline and management have more to do with keeping control of yourself than they do with keeping control of students. The teachers we know who have well-ordered classes first have well-ordered thinking and well-ordered actions. One of their first tasks is to establish authority and legitimacy with their students. Before they act like educational leaders, they consider how they must earn the right to be classroom leaders.

Discipline and punishment are not the same thing; in fact, they are very different concepts. Discipline is a positive term. As we have suggested earlier, it is easy to identify mature students as human beings. They are self-disciplined. We also think it is easy to tell the best teachers from the worst teachers. The best teachers are those who help their students achieve self-discipline.

> **"Permissiveness is for disciplined people."**
> - *Unknown*

For them, it's both a philosophical and a practical matter. It's the right thing to do, and it works. Why does it work? Because once students believe in and work from the basic principle of their own self-discipline, you don't have to constantly be on top of them. They are on top of themselves.

Unlike discipline, punishment is a negative term. Punishment means that someone has done bad things and you are going to do bad things to them. You are going to deprive them of something important, or do something to hurt them, get their attention, or teach them a lesson. Maybe you will even do something like push them out of school and, by doing so, deprive them of the best possibility to make economic or social successes of themselves.

Since we know what happens to those students who "fail" high school, we should teach them a lesson for not behaving in school. Why don't we make sure that we make the rest of their lives just as miserable as we can? Why don't we try to deny them the "good life"? Why don't we make it tough for them to find a job? Or, if they are lucky enough to find a job, make sure their salaries are well below those who do not misbehave in school. This is how punishment works. Does it make good moral, legal, social, and economic sense to you? Not to us.

In a school setting, the term punishment suggests that you, as a teacher, are going to be actively in charge of working to control the actions of your students. You are going to make sure that they learn a lesson. To make sure, you are willing to deny them, or hurt them (make life tough), or just move them out of the way.

Too often teachers speak 'punishment' and 'discipline' in the same breath. But they shouldn't. We don't believe that discipline in a democracy should center around denying constitutional or human rights from 50% of the students. It isn't right, and it doesn't work. Instead, discipline should spring from internal controls, not from a fear of punishment.

Why did Clark become a folk hero? Partly, because North American society likes tough, macho guys. What do Charles Bronson of *Death Wish* fame, Clint Eastwood of the "spaghetti westerns" fame, *Walking Tall*, and any grade-B karate movie have in common? They play on the North American mythology and paranoia

> "To expect to rule others by assuming a loud tone is like thinking oneself tall by putting on heels."
> - J. Petit-Senn

that celebrates the actions of one tough, heroic guy who through his fearless action cleans up the town by using, essentially, the force and the thinking of a vigilante. This punishment approach is celebrated, while the discipline approach is under attack because too many people confuse democracy in schools with permissiveness.

Don't confuse our message. We are not saying that teachers should be pushovers or wimps. Teachers should be democratic, but not mean. They should discipline, not punish. This chapter suggests that teachers need to discipline by establishing authority and legitimacy. They should use these characteristics to control the learning environment of their classrooms so that students will grow, both intellectually and socially, toward a positive self-discipline.

## WHAT SHOULD TEACHERS KNOW ABOUT PUNISHMENT?

Good teachers do not try to find opportunities to punish. But this does not mean that good teachers never punish. We would be naive to suggest that punishment should never take place. Sometimes punishment is the best way to deal with a difficult situation. Sometimes punishment is the only way to deal with a difficult situation. Still, before any teacher uses punishment, there are some things that should be considered. Here are five warnings about using punishment in your classroom

**Warning One.** There are only a few good reasons to punish and you should be sure you understand what they are. Punishment is acceptable if it

1) helps prevent further misbehavior
2) helps increase or sustain the morale of the person who must conform
3) helps neutralize the deviant as a role model
4) helps protect other students from physical or psychological violence
5) helps students learn the importance of an important rule
6) is the only way that teachers can show students that they care
7) achieves justifiable long-term goals

**Warning Two.** If punishment is necessary, fairness is important.

1) Never let your anger get the best of your good sense.
2) Never pick on students you don't like.
3) Never hold students responsible for actions that they cannot control.
4) One measure of fairness is appropriate recompense. It is difficult always to understand what motivates a student to act as he or she does.
5) Sometimes students simply do not understand that they did something wrong.

**Warning Three.** A behavior can be made worse by using the wrong kind of punishment on the wrong student.

1) You may humiliate a student in front of peers.
2) Some students are not prepared for punishment, even if they did wrong, and you may make an enemy forever.
3) There is always the chance that you might punish the wrong student.
4) It is difficult to understand and measure the correct weight of the punishment as it applies to the "crime."

5) Punishment itself encourages students to think that they have committed a crime. Once you are treated like a criminal, you start to act like a criminal.

**Warning Four.** Punishment may have negative effects. The punishment can

1) provide sympathy to the offender if a teacher overreacts
2) cause students to avoid us and to break communication that we have worked hard to build
3) cause retaliatory behavior
4) hurt a student's self-esteem
5) model behavior that is undesirable
6) eliminate behavior that is both good and bad
7) become so powerful that it becomes the only way students will respond to direction
8) set a conflict metaphor within a classroom

**Warning Five.** Punishment may have some unexpected and negative academic results.

1) Punishing a student for talking in class may cause him or her to quit working altogether.
2) Some of what we consider punishment may actually reinforce anti-academic behavior (i.e., sending students to time-out rooms provides an opportunity to daydream).
3) When teachers use additional academic work as a punishment, students may come to associate their bad feelings with the academic work rather than the punishment.

## HOW CAN YOU KEEP ORDER IN A CLASSROOM WITHOUT UNDUE RELIANCE ON PUNISHMENT?

Some teachers only know how to punish students. But we have just finished a long argument pointing out that punishment doesn't work very well; and even if it does work, the negative effects may, in fact, be worse than the misbehavior that is being punished. Some of you have formed some pretty fair questions at this point: If punishment doesn't work, does anything work? I have to keep my class in order, don't I? Is there some way to have a classroom that runs smoothly?

To all these questions, the answer is yes. You need to build a classroom that works. But, to repeat, punishment is the worst way to build the classroom you want. A smoothly running classroom reflects these four basic characteristics of the teacher.

1) A good teacher has technical competence in establishing rules and consequences. Good teachers know the importance of establishing their rules and pointing out clearly the "what" and "why" of the consequences of breaking classroom rules. They also know how to act when the rules have been broken.

2) A good teacher has good rapport with students. Good teachers know how crucial communication is to the workings of the classroom. They know how to talk to kids.

3) A good teacher has good daily and weekly lessons. Good teachers know that if anything good is going to happen in class, the chances are it will not happen by accident. Good teachers plan both content and social experiences for their students.

4) A good teacher has sufficient knowledge of content and teaching strategies. Good teachers know that they are responsible for learning and teaching a body of content knowledge. But they also know that the content is not all they teach. They also need to know how to teach it. They work hard at both by reading, noting, planning, saving, and considering their own ideas and the ideas of other teachers.

## WHAT IS THE CONCEPT OF LOW-FORCE STRUCTURE?

While it is useful for teachers to know and understand how external structures encourage them to behave, or to not behave, in particular ways, our theory for this book has always been that internal structures are more crucial in organizing and managing a classroom than external structures. It is true that external forces can shape a classroom in particular ways. Still, we believe that what the teacher thinks and how the teacher acts are the two most important organizing structures in any classroom. Outside forces should not be ignored, but they should also not become the rationale for what goes on in the classroom. When the door shuts, the teacher is in charge.

> **"Children can stand vast amounts of sternness. They rather expect to be wrong and are quite used to being punished. It is injustice, inequity and inconsistency that kill them."**
> *- Robert F. Capon*

We want to help you come to be more in charge of what goes on in your classroom, without making your actions the focus of the whole classroom. To do this, we want to introduce an idea that we have structured as a principle for our teaching. You might not have heard or thought about it before, but it is central to how we think about our jobs. We call the idea "low-force structure." Low-force structure is centered on the belief that there are dozens of little ways a teacher can control or manage the classroom without using his or her mouth (yelling, screaming, forcing) or heavy-duty rules (turning the classroom into a totalitarian state). Teachers should not have to yell at kids all the time to enforce a set of rules, nor should they have to become dictators.

Central to this idea is the belief that yelling at students or setting a concrete series of mind-numbing rules is counterproductive. Both yelling and external rule setting encourage "bad feelings" and conflict between teachers and students. They retard students' growth toward self-discipline, and in the long run they do more harm than good. The idea behind low-force structure is that discipline and classroom management are always part of a teacher's thinking. They do not happen before instruction takes place (as in "sit down and shut up and then we will begin"), but they are an important consideration when planning for instruction and they happen at the same time that instruction is taking place.

> **"The graveyard is completely ordered because absolutely nothing happens there."**
> *- C. J. Friedrich*

For example, these are some basic low-force structure questions a teacher can ask:

1) What will the students be doing when I am doing what I'm doing?
2) What are the possible things that could go wrong with this lesson plan, and how can I act beforehand to prevent these problems?
3) What do the students like and how can I make what they like to do an integral part of what I do?
4) How can I mix and match activities so that the outside environment (the time constraints, the recent history of the classroom—like holidays, recent difficult assignments, or the particular problems or strengths that students have) are considered in the structure of activities?

These questions consider potential and important aspects of the classroom before they become significant problems. It is almost like a diagnostic check for cars. Instead of trouble-shooting when things go wrong, hoping to find the problem and solution, low-force structure takes time to fix things that are showing stress before the stress causes a rupture.

The idea of low-force structure works on the premise that it is easier and a whole lot less painful to prevent discipline problems than it is to fix them after they are broken. Maybe the key concepts of low-force structure can be wrapped up in the simple statements: (1) Don't do stupid stuff! and (2) Do the smart thing before it's necessary!

Here are some areas and examples focusing on physical arrangements where low-force structure can work well.

**Do's**

1) Make sure that all students have enough space to move without being constricted. For example, if kids are constantly bumping into each other, how can you expect them not to cause disruptions?

2) Think about the way you want to teach and structure your class-room accordingly. For example, if you want to lecture or give notes, make sure all the students can see you. Or, if you want to use groups, make sure that groups can work undisturbed.

**Don'ts**

1) Don't clutter your classroom with unnecessary furniture.
2) Don't make access to materials so difficult that students disturb others to find what they want.

## A FINAL WORD

Smoothly run classrooms where students are highly involved in learning activities and which are free from disruption and constant misbehavior are not accidental. Good learning environments exist where teachers have a clear idea of the classroom conditions and student behaviors that foster such an environment. Such behaviors and conditions only come about through the hard work of teachers.

## READINGS FOR EXTENSION AND ENRICHMENT

Butchart, Ronald E, Ed. McEwan, Barbara, Ed. (1998). *Classroom Discipline in American Schools: Problems and Possibilities for Democratic Education.* Albany, NY: State University of New York Press. Explores the democratic, moral, and political perspectives of classroom control.

Fuhr, Don (1993). Effective Classroom Discipline: Advice for Educators. *Nassp Bulletin, 76* (549), 82-86. Article asserts that top performers in administration and teaching understand and practice effective discipline by reinforcing and building on student's strengths.

Gartrell, Dan (1995). Misbehavior or Mistaken Behavior? *Young Children, 50* (5), 27-34. Discusses the advantages of using developmentally appropriate guidance as a method of classroom management.

Kohn, Alfie (1996). *Beyond Discipline: From Compliance to Community.* Alexandria, Virginia: Association for Supervision and Curriculum Development. Calling into question many of the assumptions underlying classroom discipline, this book offers an alternative vision to traditional classroom management models.

Lewis, Ramon (1997). *The Discipline Dilemma: Control, Management, Influence* (2nd ed.), Victoria, Australia: Australian Council for Educational Research. This book offers teachers three different discipline styles and provides guidance in classroom management, discipline strategy, and flexible problem solving.

**E**XPERIENCE *is a hard teacher because she gives the test first, the lesson afterwards.*

**- VERNON SAUNDERS LAW**

What is teaching? How does it get done? These are not easy questions to answer. Teaching is more than the sum of its parts. It is more than a perfect lesson plan. More than loving children. More than maintaining discipline. More than asking questions. More than effective instruction. More than evaluating students. More than an art. More than a science.

Teaching is incredibly complex. But we hope the next six chapters will not only help you get it done but also help you "talk the talk and walk the walk."

# CHAPTER 5

# Maintaining Discipline

*THE man whose authority is recent is always stern.*

**- AESCHYLUS**

## INTRODUCTION

Classroom management depends on careful planning of classroom organization, rules, procedures, and teaching activities. Although careful planning and preparation will pay large dividends, being ready is not sufficient to sustain good behavior. You can't assume that students will behave properly just because you once discussed what was expected of them. You will need to be actively involved in maintaining student cooperation and compliance with necessary classroom rules and procedures.

## WHAT IS ASSERTIVE DISCIPLINE?

If you read educational articles about discipline and classroom management, you will likely come across the principle of assertive discipline. A teacher who uses the principle of assertive discipline works from the belief that no child has the right to prevent classmates from learning or teachers from teaching. The first job of the teacher who uses the principle of assertive discipline is to communicate disciplinary expectations to the students by clearly explaining the classroom rules. We think that the principle of assertive discipline is a good one for a number of reasons.

First, the principle of assertive discipline works because the teacher establishes expectations for behavior from the outset. The teacher then makes these expectations known, usually by posting them as written rules and by discussing them with the students. We are not suggesting that this is the first thing that a teacher does when he or she meets a class for the first time. In fact, we would encourage teachers to set a more "encouraging" atmosphere right off the bat. Disciplinary rules are, as we have already suggested, a comfortable situation for most students because they allow students to know where they stand. Most humans, and especially most students, will respond positively to legitimate and reasonable expectations.

Second, the principle of assertive discipline works because the teacher outlines the consequences for misbehavior. Outlining the consequences is positive for both the teacher and the student. It means that the teacher's reactions to common situations have been considered rather than constructed on the spot. One of the worst things a teacher can do is to discipline using knee-jerk reactions to situations. Knee-jerk reactions often are based on the "logic" of the teacher's mood rather than on a consistent rationale. As a result, they are usually

> "It is ominous for the future of a child when the discipline he receives is based on the emotional needs of the disciplinarian rather than on any consideration of the child's own needs."
>
> *- Gordon W. Allport*

not consistent. Neither are they fair. And in the worst case scenario, if the teacher becomes especially frustrated, knee-jerk reactions are dangerous. Thoughtless reactions can harm people both physically and mentally, and they can jeopardize a job and a career.

However, assertive discipline is not the cure-all for all teaching woes. Like all things, when strictly followed it may have some disadvantages. For one thing, teachers and students can be placed in an antagonistic relationship. Teachers must be careful and come to know who their students are. For some kids, facing a book of rules just suggests that once more they are in a situation that they cannot control. Assertive discipline must be tempered with other opportunities for allowing, and in fact encouraging, student input.

Second, assertive discipline when followed rigorously does not make enough allowance for individual differences. As we have suggested before in our discussion of whether consistency is fair, students are different. The same reaction to similar actions regardless of the reasons may not be reasonable. For example, we have seen students occasionally fall asleep in class. Some students just don't care. Their falling asleep is a political activity—an announcement to teachers that what is happening is worthless to them. But some students simply are in personal or family situations where they must work, where working is the most ethical thing they could do. These students ought, we think, to be granted more slack. How can teachers know what's what? By working to know their students better.

Another potential problem with assertive discipline is that its use can impede the growth of a positive rapport between teachers and students. There is no doubt that rule-governed activity is helpful because it sets out the constraints of behavior. When rules are used to mandate interactions between people in all activities, the growth of close and meaningful relationships (one of the best things that happens in teaching) can be curtailed.

There are also practical problems with using assertive discipline. For example, it can create a whole new set of things for the teacher to do in the form of extra record-keeping. As if teachers needed one more thing to do. The point is that the principle of assertive discipline can be helpful, and it's an idea that teachers should understand and practice. Like all teaching ideas, even the best one, moderation is a key. Assertive discipline should not be the only thing that teachers do. If it is, the classroom becomes management centered rather than learning centered and the classroom flow of instruction is constantly interrupted to deal with student misbehavior.

## HOW CAN A TEACHER ESTABLISH AND MAINTAIN CLASSROOM DISCIPLINE?

In reading the literature and the research, a few principles emerge as suggestions for how a teacher can establish and maintain classroom discipline. Here are fifteen points that we think you should know about classroom discipline. We call these "Principles for Establishing and Maintaining Classroom Authority."

1) **Look for simple solutions to simple problems.** You don't need a fire hose to lick a stamp. Remember, the primary job of the teacher is to teach, not to punish. Disciplinary action is productive only when the disruption caused by solving the problem is less than the disruption caused by the problem itself. It is important to separate trivial (but annoying) problems from serious problems (some bordering on criminal behavior).

2) **Change or vary behavior or activities.** The newness of a situation is sometimes enough to encourage a student to act differently. (This is called the Hawthorne Effect.) A secondary point is that the "same old stuff" can get boring.

3) **Seek to reward good behavior instead of seeking to punish bad behavior.** How you set out your task has an impact on how you perform your task. Your attitude toward your students either encourages them or discourages them. Make sure that your primary task is to find the good and reward it, rather than always being on the lookout for problem behavior. If you can encourage good behavior, you will eliminate most of the bad behavior. Most people cannot be both good and bad at the same time.

4) **The best way to have good discipline is to build an exciting and relevant curriculum.** This point considers the educational truth that one of the main causes of classroom discipline problems is boredom. Our teaching experience strongly suggests that when students are engaged in activities they like, they just don't seem to have time to mess around.

5) **Simple-to-learn and easy-to-implement discipline strategies are not likely to provide long-lasting and satisfactory results.** It's impossible to get rid of rust by painting over it. You might hide it for a while, but it will soon seek the surface. The same is true with classroom discipline. The only long-lasting classroom discipline is that which is established through learned behavior—not something that happens sometimes and not others. Remember, discipline is an educational need of the child. Teaching it should be an important objective of the teacher's curriculum.

6) **Although authoritarian approaches are sometimes needed when an activity must be stopped, one damaging effect of authoritarian discipline is the erosion of students' learning initiative and self-confidence.** No one profits from a situation that is out of control. But could it be that the conditioned, restricted, traditional school routine prevents students from accepting greater responsibility in the learning process because an external authority is directing a student's personal growth? Some people suggest that certain elements of the school (like overused bells, public address systems, and hundreds of checks and balances) cause disruptive behavior. It may be hard for students to see their own disruptive behavior as different from school-imposed disruptive behavior.

7) **Classroom structure (low-force structure) can prevent discipline problems from occurring.** No teacher, no matter how good, can prevent all discipline problems. Still, there are things that teachers can do to make problems less likely to occur. One of these is to structure the class thoughtfully. Some class structures that you should consider include

    a. the physical arrangement

    b. time management

    c. assignments

    d. clarity and redundancy of project directions

e. grouping practices

f. classroom atmosphere (the visible reflection of a teacher's personality)

g. high quality materials

8) **Public reprimand of inappropriate behavior can lead to unnecessary power struggles which teachers don't always win.** Avoid power struggles when possible. They set up an almost impossible classroom situation. Primarily, they encourage the metaphor of conflict. Once students see themselves as being basically opposed to the teacher—them on one side and the teacher on the other—the class becomes a war. The ethical point is that a war is not right; the practical point is that teachers are outnumbered.

> **"Just praise is a debt that should be paid."**
> *- old New England saying*

9) **It is easier to prevent discipline behaviors than it is to solve discipline problems.** Discipline problems will always be there, but teachers can limit the number of problems they must deal with. Repeatedly, the research suggests how much easier it is to focus on prevention than on cure. And the best way to prevent is to create a positive classroom climate—one where individuals are supported and one where curriculum is active and exciting.

10) **Teachers with excellent classroom control are those who respect students and who expect all students to realize personal bests.** Some teachers begin by looking for problems and trying to solve (squish) them. The human truth is that you find what you hunt for. It may sound simple, but don't hunt for problems. If you only want to squish problems, you will be beaten before you begin. The research suggests that teachers who are considered supportive by students are also seen by students to have positive attitudes.

11) **"Misbehavior" includes both disruptive behavior and time-off task.** (Sometimes teachers misbehave, by this definition.) Don't model misbehavior by repeatedly taking time off task. We've had teachers like this, who seemed all too willing to go off on a story-telling tangent not at all related to the curriculum. When they wanted to get back on topic, they sometimes had trouble. Teachers should be aware of the discipline situation they create in the classroom by how they function. It goes without saying that the best way to teach is to be a good model yourself. The old and wise saying is that "Most values are caught, not taught."

12) **Build your own theories about why things happen. Then work to solve your own problems and apply your own solutions.** The cause of discipline problems is an area you should think

carefully about. Here's an important fact: the four most common discipline problems noted by student teachers were excessive talking, uncooperative behavior, instructional problems and issues, and not doing work. Consider the following questions: Why do these problems occur? Are they possible or impossible to change? If they can be changed, how?

13) **Effective teaching is a two-step process: knowledge followed by practice.** The best teachers think about teaching. There is an order to good teaching. First, good teachers consider, by reading and thinking, what comprises effective teaching. Second, good teachers take responsibility for what they have learned, practice, and put what they know into effect. One of the first things a teacher should consider is her or his tolerance level. An important next step is to tell students what that level is. (If there is something that really drives you up the wall, it's important to tell your students.)

14) **A good model for discipline can help teachers implement a strategy.** Have you ever really considered the question: What is discipline? Actions, in the name of discipline, can be very different. Why? Because discipline is not just one thing. Sometimes doing one thing is correct; another time it is not. You will need to come to understand what discipline is to you. To help you, here is a simple way to define different types of discipline.

    a. Preventive discipline is used to create a positive learning environment and to set up rules and consequences.

    b. Supportive discipline enhances the accomplishments of the class.

    c. Corrective discipline helps solve further problems by democratically solving problems and helping students make good choices.

    d. Adaptive discipline is individualistic. A student is dealt with in a personal manner.

15) **The goal of discipline should be to help the student grow intellectually and learn to handle personal behavior more maturely.** One of the mistakes that many young teachers make is that they confuse quiet with good discipline. But good classroom discipline means more than keeping kids quiet. Good classroom discipline cannot be separated from the more important aspect of the growth of self-discipline. It is absolutely wrong-minded to think of discipline as a negative thing. It is one of the most positive learning experiences a human can achieve.

## A FINAL WORD

It takes a while before teachers really find out about teaching. One truth is that no university classroom or textbook can tell teachers what it's really like in the classroom. Teaching is one of those jobs where you just have to be there. One of the first things that first-year teachers learn is that life isn't always as it's supposed to be in the classroom. There seems to be an awful lot of false information being spread about teaching.

> ## "A torn jacket is soon mended, but hard words bruise the heart of a child."
> *- Henry Wadsworth Longfellow*

We have some advice about how to learn about classroom life. Learn all you can before you go into the classroom and go there with your eyes open. But if there is so much contradictory advice, which advice can you trust? Again, we have some advice: trust every piece of advice—a little. Unless it is immoral or irresponsible, reject nothing outright. But, at the same time, accept nothing outright.

You have to learn for yourself what the classroom is like. Unfortunately, some teachers never seem to learn much about teaching. Specifically, they learn nothing about kids. One myth many teachers believe is that their first job is to establish technical competence in establishing rules and consequences. This, they think, is the most important step in establishing a smoothly running classroom. But if we ask students, they tell us something else. Students state that good rapport is most important. They want teachers to know them and to be assured that the teachers like them.

## READINGS FOR EXTENSION AND ENRICHMENT

Barbour, Nita H. (1991). Ban the Hickory Stick: Issues in Education. *Childhood Education, 68* (2), 69-70. Teachers and administrators are presented with workable alternatives to corporal punishment for disciplining children.

Blendinger, Jack. And Others (1993). *Win-Win Discipline. Fastback 353*. Bloomington, Indiana: Phi Delta Kappa Educational Foundation. Establishing and maintaining an orderly classroom is a primary determinant of teaching success. This booklet presents an approach to school discipline that blends the best features of existing successful programs and current research findings.

Canter, Lee (1996). Discipline Alternatives. First, the Rapport--Then, the Rules. *Learning. 24*(5), 12-14. This paper details the basic principles of an Assertive Discipline program that involves building a rapport with students and creating a discipline plan at the same time.

Fay, Jim. Funk, David (1995). *Teaching with Love and Logic: Taking Control of the Classroom*. Golden, Colorado: Love and Logic Press.

This book describes an approach designed to teach students to think for themselves, to raise the level of student responsibility, to prepare students to function effectively in a society filled with temptations, decisions, and consequences, and to put the teacher in control.

Henley, Martin (1997). Six Surefire Strategies To Improve Classroom Discipline. *Learning. 26* (1), 43-45. Discusses six proactive strategies to help teachers improve classroom discipline.

Michlowski, Aida A. (1999). From Conflict to Congruence. *Kappa Delta Pi Record, 35* (3), 108-11. Describes strategies for peaceful resolution in the classroom including negotiation, peer mediation and arbitration.

Reissman, Rose (1993). Hot Topic. Creative Solutions to Discipline Dilemmas. *Learning, 22* (4) 48-50. Describes creative ways for teachers to handle difficult classroom discipline situations, focusing on how to deal with defiant disruptives, noncombatant noncompliers, and incessant interrupters.

Tulley, Michael, Chiu, Lian Hwang (1995). Student Teachers and Classroom Discipline. *Journal of Educational Research, 88*(3), 164-71. This study investigated student teachers' perceptions about discipline problems they encountered during student teaching and examined strategies they used to handle the problems.

# CHAPTER 6

# Providing Effective Instruction

"IT IS the supreme art of the teacher to awaken joy in creative expression and knowledge."

**- ALBERT EINSTEIN**

## INTRODUCTION

Being in a classroom alone is easy. Being with students can be downright frightening. Most of our student teachers have two over-powering fears: (1) Can I control the students and manage my class-room? and (2) Do I know enough of my subject area? Interestingly, both these fears reside in one area—providing effective instruction.

It's obvious to anyone who has ever thought about teaching. If a teacher can't manage the classroom, there can be no effective instruc-tion. It also follows that if a teacher doesn't know anything about the subject area, even if classroom control were not a problem, nothing would get taught. What is interesting to us is that the resolution of these fears is not like the proverbial chicken or egg problem. All three things—controlling the classroom, teaching the content of the subject area, and providing effective instruction—must be done at the same time. In fact, you may get tired of us saying this but it's a basic principle of teaching. The best way to ensure good discipline is to provide good classroom instruction.

When we watch teachers repeatedly, a pattern emerges. Teachers with the best classroom discipline are not those teachers obsessed with perfecting their discipline techniques. Teachers with the best classroom discipline are those who know how to teach. They provide quality instruction to their students.

Why is this the case? We have a simple theory, and it's so simple that it almost seems radical to education. In fact, we think that much of education works on an opposite principle. Here's our theory: *Children, even teenagers, want to learn. They like to work. And they hope to please their teachers.* Some of you probably don't believe this principle. You may even think we are a bit—OK, a lot—crazy. But even if what we say isn't true, let's look at the practical impact of believing that it is not true. To do so, let's take the statement from the opposite direction.

Imagine working from the opposite principle: *Children, especially teenagers, do not want to learn. They hate to work. And they hope to ruin their teachers' lives.* Think about these questions. If teachers really believed this negative principle, which we think many do, with what attitude would they go into their classes? And how would their attitudes affect the way they see what happens there? And how would their attitudes affect what does happen there? Do we have to explain farther?

Even if our principle that students want to work is wrong from the point of view of its accuracy, we would be even more wrong from a practical point of view to work from the opposite principle. As teachers, there is one thing that we have learned about people and this statement is true of most people, not just students. *People find what they look for.* We have seen this happen so many times that we cannot dismiss it lightly. When a teacher goes into class looking for trouble, that teacher invariably finds trouble.

We talk to kids often. When we talk to them about school, they generally have only two complaints. First, they hate being bored. Second, they hate teachers and schools that aren't fair. That's it. Just those two complaints. But we've heard students repeat these two points so many times that we must believe them. And it's this belief that makes us tell teachers that if they want to have good discipline they should avoid doing two things: (1) Don't bore your students (2) Don't be unfair.

## WHAT'S A CLASSROOM LIKE?

Even if you are not yet a teacher, most of you have been in classrooms all your life. In addition, you care about classrooms. If not, you wouldn't have chosen to become a teacher. This gives you a special insight, we think. Almost everyone thinks they know how classrooms work.

We think that one reason teachers have so little respect is that everybody is an expert on teaching. Because everyone was once a student, he or she believes that life in a classroom is fairly easy. We don't doubt that you have already met some of these people. These are the ones who feel they know quite a bit about how teaching should be done, even if they are not teachers. They are also the ones who feel they have a special obligation to tell you.

The truth is those people really don't know as much about life in classrooms as they think they do. Most people have never really thought about what goes on in classrooms. We mean about what really goes on in classrooms. Thousands of things go on in classrooms; but basically, a classroom is a place of interaction. And a classroom has two interacting dimensions. One dimension includes the work of the teacher and the students on the curriculum, or the subject-area task that is being covered. The second dimension is the interpersonal dimension, the relationships between people.

Because these two dimensions exist simultaneously, the teacher's role is multi-dimensional. A good teacher needs skills and knowledge about the subject matter and a good teacher needs skills and knowledge about how to react to classroom events. But it isn't enough just to have these skills and knowledge. For those who don't live in classrooms, there is a surprise when they visit. The most interesting thing about a classroom is how quickly things happen. If one were to use a sports metaphor, teaching is probably more like hockey or even roller derby than it is like baseball or golf. There is much planning necessary before a teacher begins to teach, but once the teaching hits the fan there is a constant flurry of activity that teachers must keep up with and control. And you wonder why teaching is tough!

But the whole environment is complicated by one extra piece of information and this is the most complex part of the classroom. Teachers are not the only people in the classroom. It's not just the teacher who must control what's going on. Both teachers and students must constantly monitor and interpret in-class behavior so that

> **"You may give them your love but not your thought, For they have their own thoughts."**
> *- Kahil Gibran*

they can make decisions about what is occurring, both academically and socially. Then, they must act. This is the real complexity of the classroom. Everyone in the classroom is part of the activity.

Both instructors and students watch and listen to what is being said and done (including those task-related bits of information, usually called directions) and how it is being said and done (voice tone, inflection, body posture, etc.). They then make sense of the classroom by coloring what they see and hear with their own personal interpretations of what the activities mean. To both students and teachers, events are more than simply information; they are mental constructions that influence subsequent behavior.

## THE DARK SIDE OF INSTRUCTION:
## WHEN THINGS GO WRONG

We wish that every part of teaching and school were glorious examples of the best of human relationships and human dignity. We wish that all teachers could teach, and that all students would learn. We wish there were never problems. But, unfortunately, there are problems. And these problems are especially devastating to classrooms. They cause breakdowns in both the task orientation (the curriculum assignments) and in interpersonal interactions and relationships. It is true that good teachers increase in their skills of handling the potential problems of schooling as they gain experience, but it is also true that no teacher we know has ever been able to avoid the looming potential of problems.

We are going to make some suggestions about how better to handle some of the problems you might face, but before we do we'd like to offer some possible reasons why problems exist. One thing you should remember as a teacher is this: **all problems are not your fault, but they are still your problems.** Some problems are inherent within the structure of school itself; some are problems

> ## "A captive audience is rarely captivated."
> *- Unknown*

particular to a single school, classroom, subject area, or student. And while we hate to admit it because it might scare good people away from teaching, sometimes teachers are powerless to overcome all the problems they face.

Research suggests that some causes of violence in schools are social problems that originate in the community in which the school lives. Some of these problems might include: 1) poor town or school board planning (i.e., long time periods spent on buses can cause resentment among students), 2) the cultural differences of students (cultural misunderstandings are some of the most difficult to overcome), and 3) the variety of different life styles that families live (for example, students whose families live in poverty have a more difficult time in school than students whose families are well off).

Some of the problems of particular schools include: 1) inadequate facilities (i.e., sharing textbooks only encourages students to goof around and provides a strike against a student's ability to concentrate), 2) contradictions within the school (i.e., students who are told not to interrupt, but get mixed messages when they are constantly in the middle of school-based interruptions like bells, loud-speaker announcements, and phone calls to teachers), 3) out-of-date curricula (i.e., beaten up textbooks or curriculum with pieces missing slow down learning), 4) rigid organization (i.e., administrative dictatorships squelch the life from students), 5) overcrowded classes (i.e., it's hard to work when you're sitting on top of your neighbor), and 6) inappropriate teacher training (i.e., among other things, teacher education courses are often guilty of setting up a relationship of conflict between beginning teachers and students).

How can these problems be overcome? It would be terrible to list a series of problems, and then not be able to offer solutions. Still, we admit that the specific problems of your classroom will need specific solutions that we cannot offer here. However, our experience as teachers and our reading of the research allow us to offer some general solutions to many of the problems you might face. These solutions are global, or general, in nature. To make our suggestions work, you must ask some important questions like "What do they mean for me and my specific situation?" "How do they encourage me to use what I have going for me (my personality, my knowledge, and my talents) to make the changes I need to make?" And, "What do these general suggestions mean for the particular students that I am working with right now?"

With these questions firmly in your head, here are some general suggestions from our experience and the research literature:

1) People within schools should attempt to construct schools and school learning so that it is closer to real life.

2) Good curriculum should offer students opportunities to mature and should encourage them to grapple with responsible decision-making. Good curriculum should also encourage cooperation between students and between students and teachers.

3) Teacher education (including university courses and teacher in-service sessions) should help teachers learn to cope with changes in pupil and parent attitudes as well as with changes in curricula.

As we have stated, these are general suggestions. We encourage you to think about them. How they are worked out within particular schools, school districts, and within particular teacher education faculties is an important matter.

## WHAT DO YOU NEED TO BE A GOOD TEACHER?

Before trying to answer this question it is important to know why some teachers are not good teachers. Some books would lead you to believe that, with a few skills and some hard work, anyone can become a good teacher. This simply isn't true. Not all people can become teachers. Some teachers are not good teachers because they just don't have the basic skills or the personality to be a good teacher. Some teachers are not good teachers because they don't want to be. They simply are not willing to work hard enough to become good teachers, or to work hard enough to overcome their specific problems.

We think the following generalization is true. All teachers have unique problems that they must work to overcome. It is how hard you are willing to work to overcome them that is a key to your success as a teacher. For those of you who really want to become good teachers, there are a number of simple requirements. They include a knowledge of

1) subject area
2) teaching methods
3) organizational techniques
4) communicative devices

The requirements of good teaching may be simple to list, but they are not simple to achieve. In putting this book together, we have kept in mind the following idea: it is easier to say what teachers need to do than to tell them how to do it. Becoming a good teacher takes work, much of it. As we have said before, becoming a good teacher also takes a knowledge of the school and what happens there.

## HOW DOES INSTRUCTION TAKE PLACE?

We have briefly suggested what classrooms are like. Now it is time to suggest how instruction takes place within the school. Basically, there are two overriding instructional strategies used in schools. One strategy involves making the unfamiliar familiar. This strategy is most appropriate at the elementary level and involves work at what Piaget called the concrete operational stage. The second strategy involves making the familiar unfamiliar and is most appropriate at the secondary level. This strategy involves work at what Piaget called the formal operational stage.

When teachers work to make the unfamiliar familiar, their first important task is to match the difficulty of the material to the ability level of the child. Completing this task works best if the teacher assumes that the student is "ignorant" of what is being taught. A second important task is to figure out just how well a student is learning the material. Just how thoroughly are the students to learn the content set before them?

When a teacher is working to make the unfamiliar familiar, there are a number of common tasks the teacher can use. Pointing and naming are the most common. This may all sound theoretical, we suspect, but think about how many ways a teacher can "point and name." Ask the question: "How can I teach my students the material that they should know (according to the program of studies or curriculum you are required by law to teach), but do not know." In the practical answering of this question, the task becomes more simple.

Textbooks are pointing and naming activities. Field trips exist to make the unfamiliar familiar. Films, records, television programs, flash cards, stories, and pictures all expose children to aspects of the world they may not have known before. They may help children who already know something about a topic understand it fully or in a new way.

Pointing and naming are important aspects of any teaching. They increase your students' knowledge, first of things they have not known and second of things they may know a little about but do not fully understand. For example, children may have heard about nuclear war, but may not understand the political situation of the world that led to the development of nuclear warheads. In such a case, pointing and naming can increase more than their knowledge. It may also work to increase their anxieties as well as their comprehension.

The second type of teaching, more familiar to the higher levels of schooling, is to make the familiar unfamiliar. The theory of making the familiar unfamiliar rests on a simple principle: there is a mismatch between the student's level of thinking and the depth of the material being studied. In other words, students may only have a surface level understanding of issues such as racism, the politics of medical research, poverty and hunger in the world, the impact of sports on their communities, or materialism. The list could go on and on. The central task of the teacher, seeing this mismatch, is to motivate original thinking and problem solving. By making something that is familiar unfamiliar, teachers can expose hidden potentials and stretch the learner's mind to challenge what it has, up to this point, taken for granted.

Again, this may sound theoretical. But there are certain kinds of activities that achieve the purpose. Poetry or music are probably the two activities that most students know best. Young people love their music, as recent North American research studies point out. A study of the nuances of words or musical lyrics and videos can show how familiar language can be used to mean new things.

Exploring the meanings of language or pictures is one way to help students see hidden ideas. A study of the context of the art form

> **"Language is by all odds the most subtle and powerful technique we have for controlling other people."**
> *- George A. Miller*

or the photograph can highlight the hidden meanings and aspects of the artist. A study of the political and historical situation can highlight the ideological background of the participants. The simple truth about knowledge, and it is true for all subject areas, is that knowing the facts is not always knowing the truth. Facts are like numbers in mathematics: they can be added up wrong.

## HOW DOES COMMUNICATION
## TAKE PLACE IN THE SCHOOL?

Because humans talk to each other all the time, there is a tendency to think that communication is easy. One of the biggest problems our students have when writing lesson plans is that they don't attend to the building of communication. They will often write a long outline of points, and then state tersely: discuss the points. But they don't think, or at least they don't note, just how they will provide for their discussion.

Communication is not always easy. There are two forms of discourse in schools, ideological and educational. In everyday language, teachers communicate values and ideologies at the same time they are communicating content.

Think of some of the teachers you have had in the past. Name some that you liked a lot. Then name some that you didn't like as much. Think about these teachers and their communication patterns. You may discover an educational truth: teachers are defined by and perpetuate these two forms of discourse. If this is the case, it is important to think about not only what you will say (content) but how you will say it (ideology).

Good teachers have good communication patterns. Those who study communication suggest that there are four dimensions to good teaching communication: (1) extroversion, (2) composure, (3) character, and (4) competence.

First, some have suggested that the best teachers are the best actors. Maybe there is an essential dramatic role teachers must play. Surely good teachers can't hesitate or be afraid (don't confuse fear with a healthy dose of the "butterflies") to get up in front of a group of students. Second, good teachers can hold it together in the face of pressure. Third, it is possible to be a good baseball player and a bad person, but most good teachers are also good people—character people. For most teachers, it would be hard to separate their own personality from their teaching personality. Fourth, good teachers know what they are doing. They have a positive self-image. This positive self-image helps them establish credibility. Teachers who "know their stuff" both seem and are more competent.

> "Small children know more than they can say. Adults say more than they know."
> - *Unknown*

There is a difference between a teacher who thinks he or she knows all the stuff and one who knows some of the stuff well and is learning some more. Nobody knows it all. To pretend to know it all is arrogant. Furthermore, working to know everything is "practically impossible" for young teachers. But it is possible to learn some of the stuff very well and to be extroverted, composed, and competent about that stuff. Character shows itself in your pursuit of knowledge and as you work in class interactions.

Research shows a high correlation between anxiety and teacher warmth: as a teacher's anxiety increases, the teacher appears less friendly and responsive to the students. The more anxious the students, the more critical they are of teacher performance. Teachers appear enmeshed in a teaching-learning cycle in which anxiety and performance (both teacher and student) play off against each other.

This is, as Spock would say, imminently logical. A key is to know that this negative correlation between anxiety and performance can be turned around to work in your favor. If you know that there is a high correlation between student anxiety and teacher and student performance, then ask: "How can I, in very practical and legitimate ways, help reduce anxiety? What would make me anxious as a student?" We see too many people trying to increase anxiety as a way of forcing kids into learning. It's a stupid thing (impractical, because it doesn't work) to do!

### HOW CAN TEACHERS MOTIVATE STUDENTS?

We have already suggested that good teachers present challenges to their students. But there is more to good teaching than presenting challenges. Good teachers also motivate their students to reach the challenges they put out.

Research suggests that there are a number of important principles for motivating students. They can be summarized into five suggestions:
1) Invite success.
2) Have high expectations.
3) Work in cooperation, rather than in conflict. Cooperative learning is especially effective with young people who generally lose in competition.
4) Set out the learning tasks carefully and fully.
5) Interact with students. How a teacher handles and encourages responses can lead to increased involvement and interest.

### WHY IS DECISION MAKING SUCH AN IMPORTANT TASK?

We have suggested that learning decision making is crucial to the intellectual and social maturity of students. But teachers also benefit from being good decision makers. Instructional effectiveness is not determined simply by what expert teachers do, but by the ways they decide what to do. Good teachers are also risk takers. They know that they, too, must risk if they are to learn more about teaching. They know that their pedagogical intelligence is developed by confronting instructional dilemmas and trying to use their understanding about the classroom milieu to solve problems.

Beginning teachers already know this, but people don't know everything they need to know when they first hit the classroom door. In fact, first year teachers are wonderful because they are so inspired and enthusiastic. But the truth is, they don't know much about being good teachers. They lack experience.

Experience is more than just time spent. Experience is only useful if it is considered and used to learn. Maybe the most important truth about good teachers is that they learn from their experiences. The constructive use of experience is a crucial factor in good teaching. The classroom is almost a whirling dervish, always almost out of control, but not quite. Teachers can think about what is going to happen before they meet the challenges, but the pace of the classroom is another kettle of fish.

Things in a classroom happen so quickly that teachers must often rely on intuitive knowledge in making decisions. Where does intuition come from? Intuitive knowledge is gained from previous experience. Good teachers consider a variety of things in making any classroom choice. What they do fits the situation at hand, the context of the situation they are facing. Just repeating what someone else did once that seemed to work is no assurance that the correct action will work in today's situation. Replicating this behavior without regard for context offers no assurance of appropriateness. In fact, it almost insures lack of appropriateness.

Part of intuition is coming to know your own strengths. Good teachers are able to utilize their own strengths and take alternative means to the same end. Context clues can influence instructional decisions, but good teachers can "reach back" into their own experience and find the almost unconscious interpretations of earlier encounters that are

> **"Practice what you teach."**
> *- Unknown*

similar to situations they are presently facing. This "reaching back" allows them to infer a whole list of potential solutions to the problem at hand. They are then able to consider these choices, almost in a matter of milliseconds, and decide on the run. This, for good teachers, is the meaning of intuition.

Research suggests some factors that influence the decision making of experienced teachers. These include (1) beliefs about teaching, learning, and the role of the teachers in problem solving; (2) teachers' perceptions of individual students; and (3) teachers' psychological and emotional needs.

We mentioned what students need earlier, but what do teachers need? Like all other humans, most teachers seem to need to feel that they are doing okay and that they are in control of their situation. Not doing well or not being in control can drive a teacher to drink. Teachers act as they do for a number of reasons. Sometimes teachers have "pets." Like all other humans, they like some people better than others. When we were young teachers, it used to eat us up and keep us awake at night that we didn't like all of our kids the same. We would say about some kids: "If these were grown-ups, I wouldn't have anything to do with them. But these kids are in my class and I must work with them no matter how I feel."

Teachers are also not free of social biases. For example, a teacher's social origin can strongly influence how he or she will react to the status attributes of their students. If you know that you are like other humans and can be influenced by outside pressures, there are some things you can watch out for.

In particular, the research suggests that students with little status or who are members of a minority group experience their greatest difficulties in the classrooms of high-status teachers. They have little chance to succeed because their teachers hold lower performance expectations for them. And even without knowing how they are acting, their teachers score low on classroom-climate measures. Year-end marks and standardized-test scores of such students are expressed by the teacher-student social distance and teacher disaffection. This means that if you are a teacher in a low-ability classroom or a classroom with minority students, it is especially important that you monitor your feelings and actions.

One of the biggest problems of teaching is knowing that what to do and doing it are two different phenomena. This is why good teachers often have a number of years of teaching experience under their belts. For teachers just starting out, it is possible to sense that something must be done but there may be a lack of ability to do it. Many important teaching skills can only be developed with practice and experience.

Knowing that experience is an important aspect of good teaching, what can a beginning teacher do to maximize positive effects? The answer is quite simple. If you want to make a change, be well prepared before you enter the classroom. Achieving control means to first take control of yourself, then to take control of the situation.

## A FINAL WORD

Although many of the skills of good teaching are transferable, being a good teacher in elementary school is not exactly like being a good teacher at the junior or senior high school level. This is because the tasks of teaching at different levels vary. Balance and variety are stressed at the junior high level. Coverage is stressed at the senior high level.

One reason why teaching tasks differ with each level is because the students differ. Research studies show that, as adolescents mature and move through school, their concepts of what constitutes effective teaching change. For example, in grade six authority and responsibility for learning are anchored to the teacher. By grade eight, students may no longer expect the teacher to always tell them what's what, but they do expect the teacher to be sensitive to their individuality. As students grow older, their link to the teacher becomes one of personal like or dislike rather than one simply based on status. For example, by grade ten, students indicate that they are apt to dislike or even distrust teachers who they think are impersonal and controlling. By grade twelve many students describe the teacher in terms related to teacher empathy towards them and their empathy towards the teacher.

## READINGS FOR EXTENSION AND ENRICHMENT

Adams, Arlene (1999). *Handbook for Literacy Tutors: A Practical Approach to Effective Informal Instruction in Reading and Writing.* Springfield, Illinois: Charles C. Thomas, Publisher, Ltd. Aiming to make the literacy tutoring task as easy and effective as possible, this guidebook presents a set of strategies that tutors can implement immediately as they begin to work with students

Brown, Bettina Lankard (1997). *New Learning Strategies for Generation X.* ERIC Digest No. 184 (Report No. EDO-CE-97-184). Washington, DC: Office of Educational Research and Improvement (ERIC Document Reproduction Service No. ED411414). Suggests that effective instruction requires that teachers target their teaching toward the unique characteristics of today's learners.

Goodwin, Yvonne A. Kincaid, Tanna M. (1998). *Essential Elements for Developing Effective Instruction in Any Setting.* Paper presented at the National Convention of the Association for Educational Communications and Technology (AECT), St. Louis, MO. This paper offers a definition for the word "effective" and then discusses implications of research on the environment in relation to designing effective instruction.

Munson, Mark (1998). Ready for Rehearsal? *Teaching Music, 6* (1), 32-33. Divides choral teaching into four steps: analysis, lesson-plan derivation, rehearsal, and evaluation

Parsons, Jim. (1991). *What Works.* Edmonton, AB: Duval House Publishing. A collection of "how to" ideas to make classrooms more focused, exciting, organized, creative and fun.

Wagner, Walter (1992). *Educational Technology: A Broader Vision. Education and Urban Society, 24* (4), 54-65. Considers the role of educational technology in designing effective instruction.

Wehmeyer, Michael L, Ed. Sands, Deanna J, Ed. (1998). *Making It Happen: Student Involvement in Education Planning, Decision Making, and Instruction.* Baltimore, Maryland: Paul H. Brookes Publishing Co. This book provides teachers and other practitioners with a variety of procedures and materials to help students with disabilities become involved in their transition planning to the maximum extent possible.

# CHAPTER 7

# Creating a Positive Classroom Environment

**W**ORDS but direct; examples must allure.

**- WILLIAM ALEXANDER**

## INTRODUCTION

One of the most important jobs any teacher faces is setting up the environment in which he or she will work. A classroom is more than a room with chairs and desks. It is a personal reflection of the teacher who teaches there. It is the place where a teacher lives and works. Classrooms are one of those educational commonplaces that most people believe they understand, but do not understand fully.

It is not hard to read research studies and infer suggested actions. We know some things about how classrooms work. There are things teachers should know about classroom organization and interaction. Notice that our focus is on what "good" teachers do.

## DOMINANCE

Good teachers play a dominant and a central role, but involve students in planning and organizing. There seems to be a confusion between what is often called democratic teaching and a teacher's unwillingness to control and structure. Democratic teachers allow students to have a say in the events and structures of their lives. But this doesn't mean that democratic teachers are wimps who won't stick their noses into the action.

Good teachers know that in any working classroom someone has to be in charge. The buck must stop somewhere. Someone must take the responsibility for the final choices that are made. For obvious reasons, that person must be the teacher. But the person who takes the final responsibility doesn't always have to make the final decision. In fact, good teachers know that growth in the ability to engage in constructive decision making is growth in intellectual and social maturity—part of their mandate in teaching their students.

## FEEDBACK

Good teachers provide immediate individual feedback. One of the most important reasons why teachers must assume final responsibility and control over the teaching and the environment is that the psychological and emotional development of children (from grades 1 to 12) insists on it. Good teachers know that most students get confused when they aren't sure what's going on. They also know how students typically react to confusion. Not very well. We suggest that teachers take the opportunity to provide systematic, immediate, and constant feedback. Keeping on top of things simply eliminates many teaching difficulties before they become problems.

## SHAPING STUDENT RESPONSES

Good teachers shape student responses toward the correct response. What are the signs of an intellectually mature person, a person who is a good learner? Good learners share one general characteristic: they are confident enough about their own abilities to take risks. Extending oneself by risk-taking is the single most fruitful activity that encourages intellectual growth. Students grow in confidence as they dare to risk and experience success in the process.

Teachers can play an important part in the growth of risk-taking students. Have you ever met someone (a teacher, a coach, an in-law) who, whenever you risked enough to say something, found some fault—no matter how big or small—in what you did or said? What was your reaction? If you are a normal person, you probably shrunk back, got smaller, became less willing to risk again.

Compare your reaction to the situation where there was someone (again a teacher, a coach, an in-law) who, whenever you risked enough to say something, found something positive—no matter how big or small—in what you did or said. What was your reaction? If you are a normal person, you probably felt more comfortable, became bigger, more willing to risk again.

We'll say much more about working from success later, but for right now we want to point out that good teachers are special people with a special attitude. They look for and find something positive— no matter how big or small—in what students say. Good teachers have a goal. They know they are molding students, learners, people who are willing to risk. They know that every learning experience involves some risk. It's quite simple. No risk, no learning.

## TASK INVOLVEMENT

Good teachers maintain task involvement. Good teachers know when to work and when to play. They also know when to make work play. There seem to be two mistakes about how to approach a classroom. On one end of the spectrum, some teachers seem to believe that they need to be monsters. If they can prove to kids that they are big and mean and willing to punish, they can almost assure that their students will not dare to cross them. Then they can get down to the real job—teaching. We understand their logic, but we think that these teachers are abusive.

We're not saying that these teachers always act for the wrong reason. The fact is many sincerely believe that their abusive actions help create the atmosphere that is most conducive to learning. The research, common sense, and our collective experience would pass this judgment on their efforts—not productive!

> **"We are often searching for better answers when we should be developing better questions."**
> *- Unknown*

On the other hand, there are teachers who make an equally disastrous mistake on the other end of the spectrum. These teachers believe that their task is to get their kids to like them. Their reasoning is simple. When people like each other, they won't do things that hurt the other person.

These teachers, too, do foolish things. They constantly give in to students' demands—about behavior, about work assignments, about classroom rules and regulations. By giving gifts, they theorize, kids will like them better. But what they fail to take into account is what took us a long time in the classroom to learn: most student requests about behavior (such as, it's more fun to mess around than to work) are knee-jerk reactions to specific circumstances. Students react to situations because they are immature, just as we would expect them to be. Like dogs pulling against their chains, they simply aren't at a stage of intellectual development where they can reason through the situation.

In the long run, as we have watched students react to teachers and have read the research, we have built our own theories about students. These theories may sound radical, but we believe that most students are more comfortable with sound, solid classroom structures than they are without these structures. We also believe that students want to learn and will respond positively to teachers' normal requests to limit their social freedom in their academic quest. What keeps them from responding positively to discipline? Only that they are young people who have not yet reached the final stage of self-discipline.

We believe that students expect their teachers to limit their behavior; and, if the teacher doesn't the students won't know what's going on. The result is cognitive dissonance and tension. The students we know respond to tension with active confusion. They become discipline problems. The result is not a good classroom experience for either the teacher or the students.

Good teachers ask kids to work hard, to stick to it, and to succeed. They push and encourage and prod and sometimes nag students to achieve. This is how they care for the kids in their classes. Good teachers do it because they know that without the push from the teacher there would be no achievement, no success, and no learning. Most students know that this is what separates good teachers from bad teachers.

## INDIVIDUALIZATION

Good teachers individualize and monitor individual progress. There are two key words in this statement: individualize and progress. It is possible to treat every student the same, but it isn't particularly fruitful. If you think about it, it becomes obvious that students are individuals. Like snowflakes, no two are alike. Each student has an individual history, an individual set of beliefs, individual needs (different for psychological, academic, and social reasons), and an individual learning style.

Many teachers believe that the vast variety of individual differences make teaching a challenge. This may be true. But these differences also make teaching a reward. You never know what to expect from students. Not only is each student different, but some individual students do different things on different days. Students are, after all, very much like the rest of humanity. Good teachers know that, to teach effectively, they must understand and accommodate the differences that they see.

> "The average child is an almost non-existent myth. To be normal one must be peculiar in some way or another."
> *- Heywood Broun*

The notion of progress is also important. Students grow and change. They are people of constant physical and intellectual movement. They are hardly ever static. Good teachers know that it is the very movement of students that provides them with their biggest motivational tool. That tool is progress.

As an educational idea, progress exhibits some important characteristics. It understands movement as a natural process of human, and particularly, student life. It is goal-oriented. There can be no progress without a destination in mind. Monty Python once did a comedy routine called "the hundred yard dash for people with no sense of direction." Without a notion of the goal, people can be moving—they might even be moving quite quickly—but they would have no sense of where they were going. Good teachers know that for students to be motivated they must know where they are going. What is the goal? It is the very movement of human life that makes the idea of progress so crucial to good teaching.

Last, to make progress is to be rewarded. The rewards may be small and they may be incremental, but rewards encourage. Encouragement, well-earned good grades, honest praise for success, the expression of pleasure—these are all the tools of a teacher who is motivating students to succeed.

## SUCCESS

Good teachers work from the metaphor of success. Good teachers understand that they cannot beat students into learning. They understand that you might modify student behavior for a moment by using the tactics of fear and repression, but over the long haul fear and repression simply don't work. And good teachers know that time is too precious to waste on activities that are simply unworkable.

Still, many teachers persist in believing that people are motivated to do their best to avoid the fear of failure and disapproval. So they scowl and talk mean. Reason: to show students that "the world doesn't owe them a living." They make difficult tests. Reason: to show kids that they must "buckle down." They send unsuccessfully completed tests and assignments home so that parents will yell at their kids. Reason: so that kids will be caught between a rock and a hard place, in a sort of "hot breath sandwich." They give much homework. Reason: to show kids how to get ready for "real life."

But fear doesn't motivate students. In fact, fear makes students quit. Why? Because students, like everyone else, can only take losing so long. Then, they either revolt or quit trying. Instead of motivating, teachers set up a metaphor of conflict—the teacher versus the students. Then they wonder why kids seem to be fighting them.

Good teachers know that there is a better way. This way is to understand that cooperation towards success is the only way to help students keep on keeping on. This better way can be wrapped up in the idea of cooperation: the students and the teacher working together to conquer the subject matter. For teachers who understand this idea, a marvelous transformation takes place in the classroom. They find that they actually like their kids. Furthermore, and even more interesting, they find that their kids like them. It isn't such a bad way to live.

## PRAISE

Good teachers praise judiciously and use little criticism. The body of recent research into the effects of self-esteem on student performance is clear. Repeatedly, studies show a high correlation between students who feel good about themselves and those who are successful in school. There is a corresponding correlation between feeling bad about yourself and school achievement. In everyday language, students who feel good about themselves tend to do well in school; those who feel bad about themselves tend to fail.

> **"Rewards and punishment are the lowest form of education"**
> - *Chuang-tzu*

The studies also suggest some things that make students feel good. These include the praise of their teachers and others. How do they receive this praise? Verbally, by using facial expressions, on their report cards, and in a host of other ways. They receive praise for doing well. An atmosphere of praise is a good tonic for problems.

Three aspects of praise are shown to be helpful in building self-esteem. First, there is direct praise. Teachers can watch for opportunities where students succeed in doing good things and they can praise this success. Second, teachers can praise themselves for doing something well. Third, teachers can provide opportunities and teach students to praise each other.

We saw recently how praise works with young people. Mini-basketball season just ended in one of the small communities around Edmonton. There are different divisions and different levels for players. At the level for 11 and 12 year-old participants, it was easy to see how different coaching styles affected the players. When the coach was encouraging, found different things to praise (even unsuccessful, but worthy, attempts), and didn't yell, the kids responded with enthusiasm. But when the coach dumped on the players, they responded in two ways. Their heads hung. They dragged up and down the court. And eventually, they didn't even bother to show up for games. We can expect the same reactions in schools.

It's probably not that praise itself is such good medicine; it's the attitude that an atmosphere of praise engenders. People want to feel good about themselves. People want others to like them. This is why peer pressure is so strong among young people. Some kids feel so little good about themselves that they risk getting into serious trouble just for the short-term feeling of "appreciation" or respect of others. Good teachers understand how people think. What they know becomes part of their activities as a teacher.

## REVIEW AND SUMMARIZE

Good teachers review and summarize. We think one of the  most underrated teaching skills is reviewing the material that students will learn. In our university teaching we teach students a concept called "creative redundancy." The concept revolves around the teaching question: how many times can teachers repeat the same material they are teaching in different ways? To use creative redundancy, we encourage a three-step process.

**Step One:** Identify the material (content) that you want or are required to teach. This process means studying the topic, the program of studies, or the curriculum and listing every "bit" of content [the vocabulary, the important people, the important dates and events, the important concepts, and the important skills] that you must teach.

**Step Two:** Turn this content into bite-size chunks that can be plugged into teaching activities. Some of the bite-size chunks and teaching activities we use are flash cards with vocabulary on them, questions and answers for gaming activities (we mimic television games and old favorites like Jeopardy, Hang-man, Concentration, Bingo, etc.), or reviews and tests for the end of chapters and units. We use many little puzzles, worksheets, or quick quizzes that can be turned into study materials later. We also follow one key idea: whenever possible we choose to have fun!

**Step Three:** Use classroom time to review the material. Sometimes we spend "regular" classroom time, but most often we encourage teachers to have activities ready so that "left-over" time (those times at the end of lesson plans that don't go as long as expected, or on school days where there are extra disruptions—like picture day, fire drill day, or assembly day) can be used. We also allow students access to the materials we (or they) create to take home to study or to use during "lag" times (those times when they are finished with their work but others are still working). We know that different activities require different amounts of time, but we believe that a teacher should never say to students: "We have only a few minutes left. If you sit quietly, we won't start anything else now." What a waste of time and a loss of good teaching space.

The whole purpose of review activities is to go over, and over again, the important content of our subject areas. It's like learning people's names. If you do it over and over, it comes naturally. We are working to help our students be successful. We give big exams, but by the time the students get to the exams, we make sure they know the material inside out. If they do, exams can be fun (things that are easy tend to be enjoyable). Plus, if they know the material inside out and do well, we have another opportunity to praise their work.

## INVOLVING ALL STUDENTS

Good teachers involve all students. Here are some sad truths about student involvement. There are students who go through an entire year of classes without saying a word to their teacher. There are also students who prepare hard for exams and who really know the material, but who have so much difficulty with certain exam formats that they can't succeed no matter how hard they try. These students are in the frustrating position of never being able to show their stuff.

We have many teaching goals. One of them is this: every student in our class should have a chance to talk every day. We don't always meet this goal, but we consider it something important to shoot for. Part of our reasoning is philosophical. We believe that in a democratic society teaching should be democratic. Our teaching is always political. We want to teach students the content of our subject area; but we also want to help produce active, participating citizens. How can teachers produce contributing citizens without allowing them the opportunity to contribute in class? This is a rhetorical question. We don't think you can.

Philosophically, we believe that all students should have an opportunity to speak and to be heard. We think that such a goal has a practical impact on what goes on in the classroom. Our experience is that students will tend to talk (they are social beings) even if we don't want them to. Why fight it? Better to give them an opportunity to do something they will do anyway on our terms rather than on their terms. To fight it is to encourage conflict. When we give them an opportunity to talk and to interact, we believe that we are helping them address a need that is common and to be expected in their age groups. By allowing interaction as a regular and planned part of our classes, we are helping our whole classroom.

Every student has the right to be an individual. All students have the need to express themselves. By allowing this expression to take place in ways that will benefit rather than tear down the activities of the class, good teachers save themselves and the other students a whole lot of grief.

## LIMITING STUDENT CHOICES

Good teachers limit student choices. We work from a principle that says that, as they grow towards intellectual and social maturity, students need to be given greater opportunities for choices and input into the activities of the classroom. However, to believe that students should have all the choices would be a perversion of this principle.

Teachers are responsible for what happens in their classrooms. This simple truth never will change.

Teachers may offer choices, but they can never permit students to choose not to participate in the content and the structure of the course. Simply put, the teacher must run the show. To allow students to have the final say would violate the trust that society places in teachers. It simply cannot be allowed to happen.

As always, there is a practical matter involved in limiting choices. Limited choices provide structure to what happens in the classroom. Here the principle of student comfort comes into effect. Students, like other humans, are more comfortable with structure than they are without it. We have seen students at all levels react uncomfortably to too many choices. Even at the university level, some students become disoriented when given an assignment with too many choices. They spin their wheels and simply cannot get off the mark. They spend so much time considering the choices that they never get to the actual assignment.

> "When parents do too much for the children, the children will not do much for themselves."
> - *Elbert Hubbard*

The same is even more true in elementary and secondary classrooms. The job of the teacher is to help the student get to and through the work assignment. Limiting choices helps students learn the skill of decision making, one of the most important skills they will learn. Limiting choices also helps the teacher stay on the curriculum target. Not to limit choices is to encourage confusion.

## HOLDING STUDENTS RESPONSIBLE

Good teachers hold students responsible for their work and behavior. What is the ultimate goal of teaching? Helping students to achieve intellectual and social maturity. What is the definition of maturity? One aspect is certainly considering the consequences and taking responsibility for the choices that one makes. Who are the most immature people we know? Often they are the people who "grow up" in environments where they are never given an opportunity to be held responsible for their own choices—where they are coddled in the name of protection. These are environments where someone else always makes the choices for them—where, even if they screw up badly, they never need to pay the piper—where they never have to take responsibility for the things they do.

Some unfortunate people are never allowed to grow. Growth is never put to them as a goal to aspire to. In the present, it is easier to be a perpetual child, to be able to demand and unfortunately get whatever you demand. We know people like this. They try the most patient of people. They bully, they pester, they use all sorts of force, they throw tantrums of various kinds, and they "think that the world owes them a living."

The central aspect of their lives is "me". They have been taught, often in the name of love, that they are the center of the universe. They believe that, when they are the kingpins, they should be able to demand and get their own way. It's simple; they have the status. Their behavior is logical. It is easy to understand how people never pushed to grow up choose not to.

These people are the real losers in life. We believe that one of the most rewarding feelings in life is to be successful on your own. To realize that you are a person with the maturity to make decisions by yourself, and to make them successfully. To trust and benefit from your own work. It is something quite special to be held responsible for your own actions, particularly in trying circumstances. "I can live with me. I am someone who has worth and importance." These are the key statements of humans with self-esteem. Teachers can encourage their students to grow toward these most wonderful and most human of feelings.

## EQUITABLE TREATMENT

Good teachers treat students equitably. We have already suggested some ways to prevent a common student complaint—boredom. The other common complaint of students is that teachers aren't fair. This complaint is often the most pressing problem that teachers have. Why? Because young people have a well-developed sense of fairness. Those of us with teenagers of our own have heard the common whine "It's not fair!" over and over again.

What's the answer? For one thing, kids have a point. We should be fair. At least we should try to be fair. Most textbooks suggest that consistent behavior and fairness go hand in hand, but that's a myth. There are times when consistency and fairness are not the same thing.

Some students have natural or developed intellectual advantages over others that would make consistent treatment unfair. Teachers who want to help their lower-ability students must often spend more time with them. There are other students with social advantages that make consistent treatment unfair. Some students have psy-

> **"A babe is nothing but a set of possibilities."**
> - *Henry Ward Beecher*

chological disadvantages. Some kids can't read. Some are painfully shy. Some are abused physically. Some are abused psychologically. Some are going through difficult times of personal and family tragedy.

Some kids simply have little money and are forced to work outside the home, sometimes as early as grade 7. Some kids we know don't get home from work until midnight, and then they try to do their homework. Would equal and consistent treatment of all of these kinds of students be "fair"? We think the answer is obvious: fairness is not blindly treating everyone the same. Fairness is generally a judicious choice that teachers make after they consider the impact of alternative actions.

## ARE THERE SOME SIMPLE THINGS WE CAN DO TO IMPROVE CLASS ATTENTION?

We're sure that you already see a pattern to this book. It's that our questions are rhetorical. We never ask a question that we can't answer. The answer to this question is yes. One cause of discipline problems is that the teacher does not focus the students' attention. That being said, how can a teacher help improve the class's attention? Here are some ideas.

1) Use the focusing principle. Get everyone's attention before beginning to teach.

2) Use the direct instruction principle. Get students on task quickly and keep them there.

3) Use the monitoring principle. Keep a constant check on student performance and behavior.

4) Use the modelling principle. Being courteous, prompt, well-organized, enthusiastic, and patient will help to produce the same characteristics in students.

5) Use the cueing principle. Use non-verbal reminders about behavior expectations.

6) Use the environmental control principle. Manipulate your classroom to improve both learning and behavior.

7) Use the low-profile interruption principle. Manage misbehavior as quietly, discreetly, and unobtrusively as possible.

8) Use the I-message principle. I-messages communicate teachers' feelings so that students can understand how their behavior affects the teacher. An I-message has three elements:
   a. description of behavior—"When you leave the room in a mess..."
   b. effect of behavior on teacher—"I have to use instructional time for cleaning up... "
   c. feeling created in teacher —"which frustrates me."

> **"If we are ever in doubt what to do, it is a good rule to ask ourselves what we shall wish on the morrow that we had done."**
>
> *- Lord Avebury, John Lubbock*

9) Use the positive reinforcement principle. Establish positive rules and expectations. Use sentences like, "Raise your hand for

permission to talk" rather than "Do not call out until you have been recognized."

10) Use the "what you have going for you" principle. All of you have special talents and abilities. If you are smart about teaching, these will become the keys to setting the structure for teaching, establishing authority, and managing the classroom. Not all of your students are the same; nor are all teachers the same. Each person has certain gifts, a unique personality, and a set of things that he or she does or does not like. Knowing yourself and utilizing what you know are key characteristics. Only then will teachers feel comfortable with themselves.

## TEACHING METHODS

Good teachers use a variety of teaching methods. Our perception of students may seem different from the perceptions of teachers you know. We have a high regard for what kids can and should do. We want to make our students work hard, but we also want them to achieve as much success as possible. Furthermore, we think that understanding what motivates youngsters is really quite simple. We do not believe that seeing teaching as a conflict between kids and teachers is either accurate or fruitful. Human relationships, even in school, do not have to be wars. In wars, there needs to be losers to be winners. No one we know likes to lose.

Here are some questions that come up repeatedly when we are talking to groups of young teachers: How can I keep students quiet so I can teach? How can I make them do what I want them to do? Here's the standard advice for teaching from "experts." "Don't smile till Christmas. Tighten up; then, lighten up!" We not only think the attitude these phrases portray is unethical, we think it's impractical. It's not right and it doesn't work.

The students we know like to work. They want to cooperate with adults and with other students. They want to do what their teachers ask them to do and they want to please the adults in their lives. The students we know have only two requests of teachers: (1) be fair and (2) don't bore us. We know that some kids aren't like those we know. But our experiences suggest that most kids are not the tyrants that adults often make them out to be.

If we are right that students don't want to be bored, it is appropriate to ask: what bores students? The answer is not very complex. Doing the same thing over and over again, without change, becomes boring. Even good things can get old. One of our theories about boredom is called "the banana bread theory." It revolves around a true story about a real kid who loved banana bread and whose mother baked two loaves. When the whole family went to town for the afternoon, the young boy had a feast. To this day, the smell of banana bread makes him ill. Even good things can turn sour.

One thing that really seems to bother students is not having a say in what is happening to them. Somebody else is always making all the rules. Somebody else is always arranging the schedule. Never being asked for your opinion can put you off. Most students we talk to say that their teachers should consider what is happening to them outside school.

One of the easiest but most positively commented upon aspects of our undergraduate university classes is our understanding that our education students have other classes that make demands on them. At the beginning of the course, we make the statement and we mean it: "Listen. We know that there are other courses that sometimes make very heavy demands on your time. When you come to a time when you are swamped with other work, tell us. We'll take a break from our assignments so that you can have an extended time to work on others. We won't not do the assignments, because we think that they are important, but we will put them off for a while until the rush is over."

Then we ask students throughout the term what is happening in their other classes. When we get wind of a hectic schedule that they face, we place a moratorium on our assignments. We might even call off a class. Students often comment about being understood. And we believe that most respond to this simple consideration by working even harder in our classes.

## A FINAL WORD

Good teachers capitalize on unexpected student wants. Good teachers make plans, but they don't let their plans stifle their actions. Good teachers work towards long-term goals, and sometimes they are willing to set aside short-term goals for the greater objective. Here's our theory about lesson plans: lesson plans are essential if nothing better happens in the classroom.

Some of our most memorable classes are those where the lesson plan has been deserted when other "golden" opportunities have presented themselves. This was not a pattern of behavior, but a special event. We remember being students. Sometimes we had teachers easily thrown off the topic. Sometimes it almost seemed as if they wanted to be led off topic, and we were all too happy to oblige. As teachers looking back, we wonder now if they were well-planned and ready to teach.

Good teachers do not allow themselves to be baited off-topic. Rather they are always aware of their final goals and are sensitive to what is going on in students' lives and the life of the school. They are also aware that there are times when the lesson plan can wait until tomorrow because there is just too ripe a teaching opportunity to miss.

## READINGS FOR EXTENSION AND ENRICHMENT

Burk, Nanci M. (1997). *Using Personal Narratives as a Pedagogical Tool: Empowering Students through Stories.* Paper presented at the Annual Meeting of the National Communication Association, Chicago, IL. Suggests that creating an empowering and positive classroom environment requires focusing on the processes of developing trust in self and others, participation and communication in the classroom.

Center on Organization and Restructuring of Schools (1992). Making Small Groups Productive. *Issues in Restructuring Schools*, Spr. (20). This is a theme issue focusing on effective small group instruction.

Flood, James et. Al. (1992). Am I Allowed to Group? Using Flexible Patterns for Effective Instruction. *Reading Teachers*, 45 (8), 608-16. Explores the use of flexible grouping to help all children experience success in reading and writing.

Gerk, Bryan, Obiala, Roberta, Simmons, Amy (1997). *Improving Elementary Student Behavior through the Use of Positive Reinforcement and Discipline Strategies.* Master's Action Research Project, Saint Xavier University, Illinois. Explores the idea that teachers who share personal narratives to promote understanding of communication concepts may help co-create a classroom culture in which students feel comfortable sharing personal stories that relate to the same concept.

Rusnak, Timothy, Ed. (1997). *An Integrated Approach to Character Education.* Thousand Oaks, CA: Corwin Press, Inc. The book teaches the principles that form the integrated approach to character education. Three vital aspects of teaching and learning are discussed.

Webb, Willyn H. (1999). *The Educator's Guide to Solutioning. The Great Things That Happen When You Focus Students on Solutions, Not Problems.* Thousand Oaks, CA: Corwin Press, Inc. This book teaches educators how to expand their teaching abilities, using positive language to get positive results.

# CHAPTER 8

# Building Inclusive Classrooms

*All of us do not have equal talent, but all of us should have equal opportunity to develop our talents.*

**- JOHN F. KENNEDY**

## INTRODUCTION

Most teachers walk a fine line. On one hand, similar to people in any job, they work hard to make their life in the classroom easier. On the other hand, they reach out to young people, helping as much as they can, knowing that the more they reach out the harder they work and the more difficult their job becomes. It is unfortunate, but teaching can be easiest for those who care the least.

We know that we have mentioned this point several times, but it's worth repeating, tongue in cheek, once again. The biggest problem with teaching is that there are people to teach. Subject matter by itself is easy. Most teachers, unless they are teaching out of their subject areas, love their content. But it's students that are problematic; and classrooms are filled with students. Students are both the joy and the bane of teaching.

Let us give you an obvious, but important, bit of information. The impact of this bit of information is incredible. Each person you will teach is different from each other person you will teach. Not all children are born with the same ability. Some are smarter than others. Some are more skilled. Some have a home environment that is richer. Some have particular and individual problems that make school difficult.

## THE RESPONSE OF SCHOOLS TO THE DIFFERENCES OF STUDENTS

Historically, schools have responded in three very general ways to student differences. Long ago, when we were primary and secondary school students, a teacher took all comers. The classroom was filled with people who came. Whoever showed up in a particular grade, or sometimes grades, was in a teacher's class. These students were equally as valuable, but not equally as skilled or able at schooling. To the teacher, this meant that instruction should be different. There were students in, for example, a grade six class that could not read at all and students in that same class who could, and had, read very sophisticated literature.

To cope with differing student abilities, teachers often organized their classrooms into groups of one kind or another. As evenly as possible, teachers created groups of similar ability in mathematics, reading, writing, spelling, or other topic areas being studied. Often, without even having heard of the concept, a teacher would organize quite complicated patterns of peer tutoring where a student with high ability in reading, for example, would work with a student whose reading ability was not as high.

> **"Education is the same, but capacities differ."**
> - Sa'di

We were in such classrooms. No formal training, as best we can remember, was given; but, those students who were the tutors - those with the highest abilities - just seemed to know what to do. Go over material, and if the tutee made an error correct it. As far as we can remember, it worked somewhat. Probably, we didn't know any different. It was just what school was like.

One of the authors remembers an intricate personal classroom ordering system where, for each subject, students were classified into the classroom chairs that corresponded to their achievement number in a particular subject. (We aren't sure how the teacher arrived at the number, but we always trusted that it was accurate.) Every chair in the room was numbered, from 1 to 30, with chair 1 being savored by the "top" student and chair 30 being scorned by the "bottom" student.

On cue, when a certain subject began for the day, students would move to take their places in the designated chairs - sort of a perverse and hierarchical "upset the fruit basket." It was a special day when the teacher announced chair changes - a source of pride for students who moved up or a grudging submission for students moving down. Although this practice would be seen as abhorrent today, this teacher is remembered as a good teacher. At the time, her actions were not considered as anything less than "the way the world operated." Of course, the person doing the remembering was lucky enough to not be in seat 30 and the view from close to the top was obviously a better memory than the view from the bottom.

More recently, schools (at least schools in which there is more than one class of a particular grade) have shunned such classroom organizing. Small flocks of "bluebirds" or "robins" or "crows" no longer nest in the same classroom. Instead, whole classes might be organized by ability. "Bright" and "able" students were put together into a classroom; students who were "less bright" or "less able" were put into another classroom.

Typically, "lower" ability groups consisted of students who were unremarkable for their skills or abilities. Instead, they were known for their behavior. They were the "behavior problems." Schools became virtual ghettos, streamed by skill and ability. And similar to any economic or social system where scarce goods and services are distributed, schools also distributed their resources. In response to the streaming of students, teachers were also streamed. Some worked with high ability groups; others worked with low ability groups. This whole system of "ghettoizing" schools was known as homogeneous grouping.

As you might detect from the tone of our writing, we are not fans of homogeneous grouping. It might seem to make schools easier to run and content easier to teach, but to us there are obvious problems. One problem is practical. Homogeneous grouping tends to convince teachers and administrators that students being taught as part of a homogeneous group are, in fact, all the same. In reality, these students are not the same. They might be together because they all scored within a certain range on a standardized achievement test, but they are far from the same in terms of needs, behaviors, histories, and personalities. To us, homogeneous grouping dulls schools to the needs of even "homogeneous" students.

Another problem is that the low ability groups became a wasteland for the stubble of school society. Research suggests repeatedly that low ability students soon become treated as low deserving students. They are given the least prepared teachers - perhaps teaching outside their own subject area - and are subjected to the lowest standards for achievement and behavior. Surprise, surprise; these students react accordingly! They remain in school the lowest number of years possible; and when they are at school they often are not at school. They skip. School isn't for them, and they quit to pursue work or other interests. No one seems too sad. If only they had come to school, we often hear people say, they would have done better. Blaming the victim, we often suggest.

Recent changes in North American society are forcing schools to transform. One important change is that educational funding is shrinking. Homogeneous grouping is expensive. Another important change is that North American democracy has been responding to the demands of its citizens for equal opportunities. Parents of low ability students, students who just years ago would have been moved into their own segregated classroom, are now demanding that their children be allowed to attend class with "regular" students. Children, physically and psychologically challenged have been added to the roles - mainstreamed - into "regular" classrooms. The North American classroom is now, more than in past years, the "inclusive" classroom.

## WHAT IS INCLUSIVE EDUCATION?

Simply speaking, inclusive education is the name for the educational movement to include children with disabilities into regular classrooms. The goal of inclusive education is to help students and staff gain an understanding and an appreciation of all groups present in local, national, and global communities. Inclusive education means including. In theory, inclusive education means that people should have a place - every person should be included - within the political, socio-economic, and education fabric of society. In practice, however, current definitions of inclusive education have become quite specialized. Not all students are included into regular classrooms. It depends on the school and the district in which you are teaching.

> "We educate one another: and we cannot do this if half of us consider the other half not good enough to talk to."
> - *George Bernard Shaw*

Inclusive education means different things to different people. Many teachers and administrators disagree with the whole concept. Not everyone agrees that all people should be included in the educational system. Even for those who agree with inclusion, there are great debates about who should be included, or excluded. Sometimes the debate is theoretical, sometimes philosophical, sometimes practical, and usually the debate is deeply emotional.

For those who care the most about inclusive education and who champion its cause, the question of whether or not to include people in the educational system hinges on the question of what the role of education should be. Should education be seen as a social mission;

or, should the role of education be seen as an academic mission. Some educators have wrestled the debate over inclusive education out of the practical and reframed it as an issue of social justice. These educators state that the "separate" education of "special" education students is not only unequal but is also detrimental to the development of all students.

## TEACHING IN THE INCLUSIVE CLASSROOM

Regardless of how the debate will be settled, there are still some things that you need to know about an inclusive classroom. As a beginning teacher, at least part of your agenda is survival. This makes the question of inclusion practical. Like it or not, your classroom is apt to be an inclusive classroom. Your job is to teach the students you find there.

The inclusive classroom differs from a homogeneous classroom in one special way - the differing needs of the students are more obvious. Individual differences hit teachers square in the face. There is no way that a teacher can pretend these differences do not exist. Somehow, some way, teachers must respond to these needs. That is the job of teaching - to respond to students' educational needs. Some students need additional care.

One obvious response to the additional care needed by students in a "regular" classroom is that teachers must learn how to make their classrooms more caring places for students. Teachers must encourage the growth of a classroom culture that provides caring while enforcing order; and, they must become part of the solution for students, regardless of whether the problems are learning, physical, or behavioral in nature. Schools must provide a curriculum of caring so that each student can have at least one school adult as a concerned advocate. That adult is typically the teacher.

## A NOTE ON INCLUSIVE LANGUAGE

A chapter on inclusive education begs a note on the importance of inclusive language. Research tells us that discrimination is still prevalent in our schools. This includes discrimination based on gender, ethnicity and sexual orientation. We believe that language is a powerful tool, because it both reflects and shapes the way students are treated in and outside of the classroom. As such, inclusive language in the classroom is one means of healing our schools and thus our society of discrimination. Sometimes we hear our undergraduate students complain about how tired they are of trying to figure out what language is acceptable today. "Why say 'letter carrier' when 'mailman' is so much easier," they ask us, and "what is the difference anyway?" The difference is big, and it is important. Too often students feel excluded in the classroom simply because the words being spoken or read fail to include them, creating barriers which can be difficult, sometimes even impossible, to break down. We believe it is important that teachers make every effort to research up-to-date inclusive language, integrate this language into their lessons, and, most importantly, model inclusive language always both in and outside of the classroom.

## HEALTH CONDITIONS

One problem with inclusive education is that there is not a consistent idea of what conditions should be considered when asking and answering questions about inclusion. So far we have spoken about inclusion as if we were discussing "special" education students with behavior problems mainstreamed into the regular classroom or students with lower academic abilities. But inclusion is inclusion. Full inclusion means that all students are included. Health conditions must also be considered when discussing the inclusion of all students into the regular classroom.

At least six categories of health conditions have implications for the inclusion of all students into the educational classroom. These conditions include: (1) "hidden" health conditions (e.g., juvenile rheumatoid arthritis, sickle cell anemia, asthma, and cystic fibrosis); (2) infectious conditions (e.g., Acquired Immune Deficiency Syndrome [AIDS], hepatitis B, and cytomegalovirus); (3) conditions which cause a child to be "fragile" (e.g., children in the final stages of AIDS, leukemia, of renal failure); (4) conditions that require the assistance of technology (e.g., children with ventilators, colostomy bags, gastrostomy tubes, tracheostomy tubes, and catheterization tubes); (5) neurological conditions (e.g., seizure disorders, meningitis, and brain tumors); and (6) body and skin deformities (e.g., amputations, craniofacial conditions, and burns).

And similar to any inclusion, the inclusion of students with health conditions impacts the whole environment of the school. Schools need actively to discuss health care and emergency medical plans, how educational teams will communicate, how curriculum will be shaped, how absences will be dealt with, what student placement considerations should be made, how orientation and technical assistance should be done, how transition into a regular classroom should be accomplished and how transportation is affected.

## BEHAVIORAL PROBLEMS

Students with behavioral problems make structural and curriculum demands on schools. Quite simply, schools must change to address the needs of these students. Students with behavior disorders usually have difficulty functioning in regular classrooms. In regular classrooms, they pose persistent problems. The teacher is stuck on the horns of a dilemma. To send the student away harms the student's learning; not to send the student away keeps the behavior problem right in the teacher's face and, worse yet, in the midst of the other students. Classroom teachers are often reluctant or unable to deal with disruptive behavior. Logic only works with the logical. Reasoning with the reasonable. Punishment can cause more problems than it solves.

How can teachers and schools respond? One way is to offer support. Almost all teachers who face behavioral problems need behavioral support of one kind or another. Sometimes the support is as simple as someone to talk to, commiserate with, or share rough drafts of ideas. Some of these informal support systems become friends for life, honest and appreciated therapy against the rails of difficulty.

Some support systems are more formal. Schools, for example, might set up behavioral support groups to help other teachers and students deal with dilemmas created when students with behavior problems act out these problems. These formal support systems are often very helpful for teachers, but similar to all school programs they need to be entered into thoughtfully. Before setting up a behavioral support project in any school, the following questions must be answered: Who is the target for support? What should the curriculum be? What are the roles and responsibilities of the people involved? What methodologies work best? What working links and support, training, and evaluation should be established? Behavioral support groups must work with the school curriculum, not outside or extra to the curriculum.

In successful behavioral support projects, the behavioral support teacher works with mainstream teachers to contain disturbing students rather than exorcise them from the classroom. Exorcism may work in movies, but in school it creates a variety of attendant difficulties. On the other hand, behavioral support projects have helped schools improve their attendance, have helped increase the use of school psychological services for consultancy, and have helped decrease psychologists' casework.

Typically, schools seem to hope that students with behavioral problems will go away. But there are other ways to deal with behavior problems. Sometimes, simply working with behavioral problems can have dramatic and positive effects. For example, research reports that when students with low grade point averages and high absenteeism rates are provided tutoring services and their teachers are offered consultation about making classroom environments less punitive, the classroom environment becomes more positive, more students complete assignments, and dropouts and suspensions decrease. For students who have experienced little success in school, as is the case with many behavioral problems, a little thing like turning in assignments can begin to spell positive changes in outlook, attitudes, and actions. We have mentioned the concept of success cycles before. When a student begins to experience some success, no matter how small, that student will often begin to do the little things that will encourage more success - like working harder. These activities will spur even further success, which will encourage other success-building activities, which will bring further success - and so the cycle turns itself out.

> "Success is counted sweetest by those who ne'er succeed. To comprehend a nectar requires sorest need."
> - *Emily Dickinson*

## APPROACHES TO CURRICULUM AND INSTRUCTION

Inclusion demands different curriculum approaches for different students. Schools may wish to treat students with disabilities as normally as possible; still, they can not pretend that students with disabilities do not have different characteristics or different needs than those without disabilities. As much as we might wish it was not so, some characteristics limit the success that students with disabilities can have when they are mainstreamed into regular classrooms.

We have noted that all students are different; however, it is also true that students share certain characteristics. For example, all students function in different ways; however, schools call on all students to function in at least four general domains. These domains are: (1) language and literacy, (2) cognitive-conceptual development, (3) psychosocial functioning, and (4) sensory-physical abilities. Each of these domains has its own set of skills, knowledges, and attitudes; and, these skills, knowledges, and attitudes in turn affect the curriculum the school or classroom must adopt and use. To consider inclusion thoughtfully, schools must think about how students function in each of these areas. Hopefully, the skills, knowledge, and attitudes in these areas can be improved through the considered use of a variety of education methods and creative curriculum planning.

The learning of secondary students with or without disabilities can be increased by structuring models of effective instruction throughout the school. The principles embodied within these frameworks and models of effective instruction - principles like establishing a positive classroom environment, keeping students actively involved, and modifying instructions - encourage more learning to take place. In short, these principles are in themselves good teaching activities that can be applied to all students in all classrooms. They work.

The inclusion of students with severe disabilities into classroom activities calls for teachers and schools to work in teams that consider three inclusion outcomes. These outcomes can be applied to both disabled and nondisabled students. These outcomes are: (1) curriculum inclusion, (2) social inclusion, and (3) learning inclusion. In a specific example, a language arts teacher and a special education teacher may work together to provide teaching support, prosthetic support, and interpretive support to a disabled student by developing both collaborative and consultative relationships with each other. When the task is too great for one teacher to do alone, often two or more teachers can work together.

## SUCCESSFUL INCLUSION

Research has also suggested that successful inclusion programs usually include the following components: (1) active parental involvement in development and implementation, (2) technical support for faculty and family members, (3) an individually designed integration plan stressing learning and socializing within the context of motivating activities that are matched to learning styles and activity preferences, (4) a peer buddy program which expands social and communicative skills in a structured setting, (5) an ecological approach to curriculum development, and (6) creative management of challenging behaviors. Research findings suggest that successful programs have certain redundant features. One such feature is the emphasizing of a contextual and social approach to teaching instead of the individualized approach that has tended to dominate the education of children with disabilities.

In many ways, students with disabilities need to be treated similar to students without disabilities. Research in the core subject areas such as mathematics, language arts, social studies, and sciences supports the belief that special education teachers need to teach effective test-taking strategies to adolescents with mild disabilities and to teach those other academic skills that enable students to cope in regular education classrooms. This list of "teachables" is little different from the list that could be constructed for any student in any classroom. It simply stands to reason that all students will benefit from instruction in these areas.

Teaching skills like interactive dialogue between teacher and student or between student and student has also been shown to provide interventions that are equally effective in promoting clarity and thematic salience in student reports and essays. In short, high-quality teaching methods tend to work with all students regardless of their abilities or disabilities. This point may seem gratuitous, but we make it for at least one reason. All students deserve quality instruction. Quality instruction also benefits the teacher. Students who begin to succeed in classrooms will change and grow. They may never become as academically, or socially, or physically skilled as other students; but, similar to all students, they can and will improve. The quality of their lives will, again similar to all students, improve. We believe this improvement is the right of any student.

## STUDENTS AT RISK - ESL

Students who speak English as a second language are often at risk for failure in school. Many of these students are in between two worlds; at home they speak and read in their native language. However, once at school they must make the transition to a new, unfamiliar language. Simply writing down a homework assignment is a big challenge for a student who is reaching to understand the teacher's quickly spoken words.

One of our student teachers tells the story of Tran, an English 30 student. Although Tran does not speak aloud in the classroom, she never misses completing an assignment, and she never misses class. She works hard every day at understanding the simplest instructions for an assignment. Yet she will probably not pass the English 30 diploma exam, simply because as hard as she tries she cannot write to the acceptable standard expected in English. She is at serious risk of failing.

We think that sometimes students who speak English as a second language are forgotten in the classroom, not because teachers intentionally exclude them, but because the students remain silent, afraid that their language challenges will label them as unintelligent. We believe that teachers must encourage their students to become active participants in the classroom. An inclusive classroom means just that, including all students and expecting nothing less than that they become full participants in the classroom. We are certain that Tran's peers can learn as much from her as she can from them, and that given encouragement, students like Tran will begin to feel worthy of having a voice in the classroom. As a result, they can and will succeed.

## APPROACHES TO GIFTED EDUCATION

Gifted students are an additional educational consideration. There have been many critical changes in gifted education over the past century. These changes have included the naming of gifted students as a different and "separate" group of students, the establishment of a credible research data base that helps provide an expanded understanding to the needs and abilities of gifted students, an expanded definition of giftedness, and an expansion of gifted programming to serve a greater number and diversity of students who are gifted. Traditionally, gifted students have been treated in a "special education approach" which is a static, one-way process. The result is that gifted students have faced a number of specific problems in areas like identification, programming, and categorical confusion.

Gifted education in Canada is being heavily influenced by movements like inclusive education and school restructuring. Ideally, in the inclusive school, instructional provisions are individualized and student-centered. Student diversity is celebrated, and teachers and related professionals develop cooperative and collaborative relationships.

> **"In the republic of mediocrity genius is dangerous."**
> *- Robert G. Ingersoll*

The research on gifted students suggests that the greatest academic gains among gifted students are found in programs that group high ability children together and provide a differentiated curriculum matched to their abilities and skills. The beneficial effect of homogeneous grouping with differentiated instruction is also evident for students of medium ability and low ability. In some ways, these research findings are a puzzle for educators. A common view is that gifted students should not be separated from their peers in regular classrooms. Instead, most teachers believe that gifted students should be taught by a teacher in an inclusive classroom. A self-contained gifted class will simply not meet the needs of gifted students. But research does not seem to support this perception. The puzzle is what to do, and how to understand, the research findings.

Most educational policies in North America seem to try to speak two ways. On one hand, they offer the promise of educating children with disabilities in regular classrooms with nondisabled peers. At the same time, they promise to provide specialized programs for the brightest and most capable students. The result is that trying to hold both decisions at once can lead to policy conflicts.

The jury is still out. Some authors contend that ability grouping is necessary for gifted children. Some suggest that gifted students should be educated in regular classrooms. Research also suggests teachers educated in gifted education demonstrated greater teaching skills and more positive classroom climates than teachers who had no training in gifted education. Gifted students whose teachers were trained to teach gifted students reported a greater emphasis on higher level thinking skills and on discussion and less emphasis on lecture and grades.

Process-based instructional (PBI) teaching models have also shown that they can be successfully applied to all mainstream classrooms that contain students with diverse skills and abilities. Process-based instructional teaching models help teachers individualize instruction by involving all students in the teaching and learning process through the development of plans for curriculum and learning activities. When process-based instructional teaching models are used in the classroom, gifted students can contribute to lessons and activities and work at their own pace and level under teacher supervision.

## HOW DO PEOPLE FEEL ABOUT INCLUSIVE EDUCATION?

Inclusion programs are being formed all across the country. However, they are not universally applied to all situations. Usually inclusive education can be found in some, but not all, schools in a district. Inclusive education usually involves some, but not all, students with disabilities. Research findings suggest that: (1) no district in Canada or the United States requires inclusion for all students with all disabilities; (2) some handicapping conditions are effectively included; (3) most inclusion programs are new; (4) there are significantly fewer inclusive programs at the secondary level than at the elementary level, and (5) comprehensive program evaluations of inclusion are limited.

Most teachers do their best with the hand they are dealt. Overall the attitudes of teachers not involved in inclusive education tend to be neutral or slightly negative, while attitudes of teachers involved in inclusion were positive. Student teachers, on the other hand, show different responses. In general, before student teaching, education students favor the idea of mainstreaming and report their willingness to teach students whose handicaps do not inhibit their own learning or the learning of others in regular classes. Research data indicate that advanced students hold more positive attitudes toward mainstreaming than beginning students. There is also a trend to report more favorable attitudes toward mainstreaming during professional preparation prior to student teaching. Following student teaching, however, there is a significant decline in the students' attitudes toward mainstreaming. To us, these findings suggest that student teachers tend to philosophically agree with the "idea" of inclusive education but are unsure when it comes to implementing it in a classroom. The job of the beginning teacher is tough enough and the extra complexity of inclusion makes it even tougher.

## HOW WILL INCLUSIVE EDUCATION SHAPE THE NEEDS OF EDUCATION IN THE FUTURE?

If inclusive education is to work, schools need to develop an agenda for a unified (regular and special) educational system. Those who study inclusive education offer a number of important recommendations. These recommendations can be presented as a series of principles: (1) all stakeholders must become responsible for the education of all students within a community; (2) a unified system of education must be structured that will help ensure the quality of inclusive education for all students; (3) all students need to have accountability standards that are guaranteed through a system of unified outcomes; (4) all educators should be prepared to educate all students; (5) funding systems should emphasize the sharing of resources; (6) site-based management is the way to build a community of learners that is responsible for each other; (7) a curriculum framework for a unified system should include dialogue about outcomes for planning and organizing schools into learning communities; (8) staff development should be provided that helps teachers consider how to restructure their workplace and foster problem solving, shared resources, and the need for continuous improvement; (9) all students and their families should have access to integrated community services at or near the school they attend; and (10) all students and staff should have access to and training in technology that appropriately supports collaborative decision making.

> **"If you do not think about the future, you cannot have one."**
> *- John Galsworthy*

## SETTING UP INCLUSIVE EDUCATION IN SCHOOLS

Inclusive education does not always work. Many factors have led to the failure of inclusion. These include a lack of planning, a lack of collaboration, and poor funding mechanisms for special education. Still, current trends indicate that schools are moving toward more inclusive practices and are attempting to educate the majority of students with exceptional needs in the regular classroom.

Restructuring schools so that they can implement full inclusion is a big job. This restructuring will demand that school leaders consider the factors that influence change. One of the most important jobs of any school that hopes to build a truly inclusive school and a school where inclusion actually works to help students is to create an atmosphere and a culture for change that encompasses the school's physical surroundings and structures, its formal policies and rules, its resources, the attitudes and beliefs of its teachers and administration, and the relationships that are shaped as a result of the curriculum. There is a lot to think about.

When expressing the vision of inclusion, schools must emphasize the importance of expanding the vision for support. If it is to work well, inclusive education must be supported by parents, students, and teachers. School leaders must also actively demonstrate their own conviction that full inclusion is positive, and they must express this conviction through their actions. Planning curriculum change and providing resources for that change involve planning and the provision of time, money, building space, personnel, and any other resources needed to educate all students in regular classrooms.

Providing continuous staff development means providing everyone involved with the knowledge and skills necessary for the successful implementation of full inclusion. Evaluation includes regular monitoring and assessment of progress. The final factor, providing continuous assistance, requires that resources and staff development are more than one-shot events and include ongoing coaching and support.

## A FINAL WORD

Clearly, inclusive education is here. Clearly, teaching in an inclusive classroom can be difficult. However, there are rewards for teachers. We believe one of the highest rewards of teaching is to help others, especially students. Teaching students with disabilities, regardless of what those disabilities are, is rewarding.

The research on inclusive education is promising. Inclusive classrooms seem to be classrooms where students can learn and grow. Certainly they are classrooms where new teachers have ample opportunities to learn their trades.

What we want teachers to remember about inclusive education is that the methodologies that work well in regular classrooms also work well in inclusive classrooms. Good teaching is good teaching. There is no doubt that the principles of good teaching may have to be "tweeked" in inclusive classrooms, but these principles do not change drastically.

> "Let the main object of this, our Didactic, be as follows: To seek and find a method of instruction, by which teachers may teach less, but learners learn more; by which schools may be the scene of less noise, aversion, and useless labour, but more of leisure, enjoyment, and solid progress."
> - *John Amos Comenius*

## READINGS FOR EXTENSION AND ENRICHMENT

Agran, M., Snow, K., & Swaner, J. (1999). A Survey of Secondary Level Teachers' Opinions on Community-Based Instruction and Inclusive Education. *Journal of the Association for Persons with Severe Handicaps. 24* (1), 58-62. Summarizes a survey of 65 secondary and postsecondary-education special educators who support both community-based instruction and inclusive education and believe that students benefit from each.

Bauer, Anne M., Shea, Thomas M. (1999). *Inclusion 101: How To Teach All Learners.* Baltimore, MD: Paul H. Brookes Publishing Co. This book is designed to help educators provide effective instruction to students with disabilities in inclusive classrooms.

Crawford, Susan Hoy. (1996). 101 Ways to Help Children Avoid Gender Bias. Portsmouth, NH: Heinemann. Offers practical tips that can encourage gender equality and avoid harmful sex-role stereotyping in the daily lives of girls and boys.

Forlin, Chris (1998). *Teachers' Perceptions of the Stress Associated with Inclusive Education and Their Methods of Coping.* Paper presented at the National Conference of the Australian Association of Special Education (21st, Brisbane, Australia, September 25-28, 1997). Study suggests that effective coping strategies are maintaining a sense of humor, making a plan of action and following it, and discussing the situation with specialist personnel.

Friend, M., Bursuck, W., & Hutchinson, N. (1998). *Including Exceptional Students.* (Canadian Ed.). Scarborough, Ontario: Prentice-Hall Canada Inc. Examines and advocates inclusion of all students as full members of the classroom. Comprehensive outline of strategies for implementing inclusive education.

Harper, C., & Platt, E. (1998). Full Inclusion for Secondary School ESOL Students: Some Concerns from Florida. *Tesol Journal, 7* (5), 30-36. Discusses full inclusion of English-as-a-Second-Language (ESL) secondary students in Florida.

Johnson, Genevieve Marie (1999). Inclusive Education: Fundamental Instructional Strategies and Considerations. *Preventing School Failure, 3* (2), 72-78. Reviews effective inclusive teaching techniques.

Lipkin, Arthur. (1999). *Understanding Homosexuality, Changing Schools.* Boulder, Colorado: Westview Press. Comprehensive text for teachers, counselors and administrators that suggests means of making schools more affirming of gay and lesbian people.

Ong, Chye Wah. And Others 1996). Asian Second-Language Educationists' Views on Gender-Inclusive English. Paper presented at the Southeast Asian Ministers of Educational Organization Regional Language Centre Seminar, Singapore. Describes a studied shift away from the use of gender-exclusive generic "he" to more gender-inclusive forms, and the shift away from the use of gender-exclusive "man" to a more gender-inclusive form.

Peltier, Gary L. (1997). The Effect of Inclusion on Non-Disabled Children: A Review of the Research. *Contemporary Education, 68* (4), 234-38. Presents research findings that indicate inclusive education promotes and enhances all students' social growth within inclusive classrooms and does not negatively affect typical students' academic growth.

Robinson, Kevin, et al. (1999). Inclusive Education: Evaluating the Educational Needs and Outcomes of Students with Severe Disabilities. *Reading Improvement, 36* (1), 35-39. Provides a guide for inclusive learner outcome activities and a review of inclusive education.

Rowan, Leonie (1997). The Importance of the Act of Going: Towards Gender Inclusive Education. *Studies in Continuing Education, 19* (2), 124-42. Reviews factors influencing the desire for gender-inclusive educational environments.

# CHAPTER 9

# Planning Lessons

*"...THE final performance which may take a minute, has been preceded by many hours of rehearsal."*

**- LOGAN PEARSAL SMITH**

## INTRODUCTION

A big shock for our beginning student teachers is finding a group of solid, good, experienced practicing teachers who state right out front that they do not use lesson plans. We have warned our students repeatedly about the importance of lesson plans. They have been given assignment after assignment that stress the values of planning. There is confusion on their part. While we make them write lesson plans, their school-based teachers seem to tell them that planning isn't important.

What do they do? Too often they try to be just like their school-based teachers. They attempt to teach without lesson plans. A few, especially those with much natural ability, enjoy some success. However, they often fall flat on their faces. Sometimes this lack of success forces them to ponder their experience and conclude that they don't have the right stuff to be teachers.

How wrong they are. Just because beginning teachers don't have the savvy of old teachers is no reason for beginning teachers to cash in the chips. It doesn't take a rocket scientist to understand that experienced teachers have practiced their craft for many years. These teachers have an edge over university students who are only beginning to teach. It's no wonder that our students can't pull off lessons like the old pros. Even our best and brightest students lack the one element that most practicing teachers have—experience.

If you are a beginning teacher and you meet an old pro who takes pride in the claim that he or she does not use a lesson plan, don't be deceived. That teacher is getting by on experience and the fact that a particular lesson or set of activities has been tried many times before. Only practice allows the old pro to get through a class period without a lesson plan. New teachers do not have the experience needed to fly by the seat of their pants. They need lesson plans.

All teachers worth their salt know what they are going to do when they go into a classroom. Without the direction provided by a lesson plan you would have to rely on dumb luck for anything good to happen. If you are a teacher, you know that you need a plan if you are to "teach" students. On the other hand, planning the lesson is not the end of teaching. Good teachers are not constrained by the "objectives" of their plans.

The classroom is dynamic. Sometimes, better things than what you have planned can occur. A wise teacher is sensitive to the possibility that new things can happen. The theory (it was mentioned in the last chapter but we feel it bears repeating) we have derived from our own experience is this: lesson plans are absolutely crucial, if nothing better happens in the classroom.

## LONG AND SHORT RANGE PLANNING

Who decides the following for each class? What content will be covered? What will the general and specific goals be? Will use be made of guest speakers, films, field trips, community resources or other special events? How much time will be devoted to each topic being taught? Which learning activities will be used? Will there be a textbook? If there is a textbook, how will it be used? If there is no textbook, what resources will be used?

> "To communicate you must know your subject and also how much of it you plan to communicate to your students."
> - *Unknown*

As you no doubt have guessed, you, the teacher, play the significant role in all these decisions. These are all questions that need to be answered as you plan. And quite frankly, much of the quality of the education you provide for your future students will be dependent upon your answers. To plan adequately, you must consider both the short term and the long term.

Long range plans usually include yearly and unit plans. Yearly plans are most often done on large calendars that allow you to see the "year" at a glance. You will find it helpful to block out the different units of instruction you will undertake by the week on your yearly calendar. In addition, look for special considerations of the school calendar that might disrupt your plans and change your yearly plan accordingly. Disruptions might include such things as report cards, teachers' conventions, holidays, student assemblies, and field trips.

For each major topic you hope to cover during a given year, you should develop a specific plan of attack—the unit plan. Units can run from a few days to a few weeks. If it is to work, the unit plan should be more than an outline of the subject matter. There are many different ways to write up unit plans. However, good unit plans should contain the following: title, goals and objectives, an outline of the daily lessons, and a scheme for evaluating.

Your unit plan might also include a list of resource materials— print, media, and people. Your unit should also include a calendar that displays the topics to be covered in your daily lessons and their approximate time slots. These time slots are particularly important if you plan on including such activities as guest speakers, movies, and field trips in your unit. All of these "special events" require much lead time to organize. Seeing them on your unit plan will remind you to meet deadlines for making the necessary arrangements.

Since unit plans are usually content oriented and do not specify activities for each day's lesson you will also need to develop daily strategies. This is short range planning—lesson planning.

## HINTS ABOUT LESSON PLANNING

We have outlined some planning strategies that we have found useful over the years. They are included in a series of suggestions that we think will help you plan for good instruction, but not be so tied to your plans that you cannot be sensitive to anything else that might happen.

1. Remember that the key question in lesson planning is "What do I really want to do?" There are always at least two things to consider before teaching a lesson. There is (1) the content you choose to teach and there is (2) the way you choose to teach. You are teaching content and you are teaching how people should interact with each other.

    When you create a lesson plan, there are key questions you should ask. What goals do you have for your group? What general principles do you follow when you teach? How do you think people learn? How do you think people should learn?

2. In lesson planning, format is an important consideration. If you are like most university students, the lesson plans you made for your classes were exceedingly long. They were filled with objectives that you wondered if you were really attending to. And they made you wonder if you could possibly plan this thoroughly for every class you were to teach.

Quite simply, you can't plan for teaching as you planned these lessons for your university teachers. These plans were most likely designed to be graded and your instructor, no doubt, wanted to see your thinking laid out in detail. In the day-to-day rush of teaching, you will never have the time to be so complete. And this statement may shock you, but even if you did have the time you wouldn't want to make these long, objectivized, complex plans. You couldn't follow them. You must have something you can use—on the spot.

3. Lesson plans should consider what you believe is crucial to education. For instance, we believe people learn better from active involvement and so our plans should involve people in their learning. (For example, we could tell you the Top 40 ideas in education and you could write them down. But how much better would it be if you created a Top 40 for yourselves?)

When making a plan, we think it important not only to know the content of the plan but to know what you want to do. We also think it is important to understand that there must be activity involved. When we come to a plan, we always ask: what are the students going to be doing when we are doing what we're doing? There are other important questions involved here:

a) Can we keep control of the situation? (If not, we don't do it.)

b) What do the kids like? (We don't always give them what they want, but why not if we can?)

c) What have we done before? (Why do the same activity repeatedly?)

d) What, from our experience, won't work? (This may seem simple, but if it doesn't work don't do it.)

e) What are the personalities of the specific people in this class? And so what? (If two students always mess around when placed in the same group, don't put them in the same group.)

f) What do we personally like or enjoy doing? (We have found that if we like something, we bring more joy to it than if we do something we don't like. And since students tend to catch our moods ....)

g) What do we believe about teaching students? (For example, we have already stated that we believe that self-esteem is important; that success breeds success; that activity, good directions, bite-size pieces work best, etc.)

4. Lesson plans must consider the curriculum. The curriculum guides the lessons you choose to teach. If the curriculum you are using is like most, the knowledge, skills, and attitudes sections here offer wonderfully rich hints for making up lesson plans. There are two reasons for knowing the curriculum. First, it is the legal tender of the teaching profession. You are quite simply required by law to teach the curriculum. Second, it offers practical ideas. Look at the verbs. Design activities that mimic the objectives of the curriculum.

5. Timing is crucial when planning. A principle we follow is to never give enough time for kids to finish. It is easier to extend time and appear nice than to cut down time and look mean. Dead space can be a killer. It's when mutinies occur.

6. Finally, we encourage you to let the students know the structure and the purpose of your teaching and your planning. In our experience as students, we had only a few teachers who showed their reasons and their purposes. Most seemed to think we shouldn't know why things were happening as they were. We feel that most students respond to honesty and openness. We encourage you to make both a part of your planning.

7. Consider the variety of your activities in your lesson plans. Make sure that many different activities are going on. Remember that you can eat too many chocolate milkshakes: even the things you love become sickening when they become the only thing you have.

8. Determine when you write daily lesson plans not to cheat yourself. Write them completely, and write them with an eye for next year. You might remember a vague

> **"Don't be more precise than the subject warrants."**
> *- Plato*

plan the next day, but there is little chance you will recall it in a year. This can be especially frustrating if you have devised a great plan, but can't remember its specifics. Trust us. You'll kick yourself if you don't write a plan completely the first time.

9. Create a planning form that you can use and that has everything you need, but nothing more. You can't use those big plans you made for your university teacher, so dump them. They were made to be graded, not used by teachers. You know what you need: (1) you need a heading that will identify the plan and where it fits in the unit; (2) you need to know by a quick look what the activity is Is it active or passive? do you need to get something ready in advance?); (3) you need to list the things

that you will do as the plan unfolds in class—these are directions to yourself; and finally (4) you need reminders about what is coming up next and what the students should do (for example, is there homework?).

10. Review the form of your plan. Reread the plan checking for things you don't understand. (If possible, find a critical friend who can tell you what can't be understood. You may be an outsider to your own thinking next year. In addition, if the friend is also creating lesson plans, you can cut your work in half and double your ability to think.)

11. Make sure you can follow your plan on the spot as you teach. Remember the head of a bean theory. We once read a Ripley's Believe It or Not that reported that there was a woman who wrote the entire Holy Bible on the head of a bean. We're sure that God blessed her devotion more than her ability to read it afterward. Don't forget your enterprise. You have to be able to work in front of the "traffic" and the group. Here are three important hints: (1) good spacing helps you, (2) numbers are easier to follow than dashes. And (3) highlighter pens were invented for teachers. (You might even create a consistent color code that warns you about what is happening in your plan. Like blue for homework, red for things to prepare, green for group work, etc.)

## A FINAL WORD

Plans take  different forms, but all can be thought of by using the same metaphor, that of taking a trip. When we talk to our students, we call this planning process "driving through Chicago." Here's how it works.

As in making any trip, we create and use three simple forms of plans. Say we are taking a trip from Edmonton to Gander, Newfoundland. Briefly, one plan form considers the whole trip from Edmonton to Gander (equivalent to the yearly plan). How long would we want it to take? How long do we have? The second planning form (equivalent to the unit plan) considers where we will stop each day of the trip. Where can we get good corporate rates on hotels? Where are there good places for the family to sightsee? And the third plan form (equivalent to the lesson plan) considers special difficulties that we will meet each day (e.g., if we were taking a route south of the Great Lakes that would force us to drive through Chicago). (By the way, the highways around Chicago are always busy, filled with construction, are poorly marked, and are toll roads that call for exact change if you don't want to wait in a long line. Always drive through Chicago on Sunday, always prepare for the toll booths by having correct change ready, and always have a good city route preplanned because of the constant construction. In short, you need to have the specifics ready.) Have a good trip!

## READINGS FOR EXTENSION AND ENRICHMENT

Cloonan, Kathie (1998). The Busy Teacher's Lesson Plan Book. Peterborough, NH: Crystal Springs Books. Offers ideas to help teachers balance their literacy curriculum.

Freed, Shirley A., Moon, Louise (1999). *The Multiple Intelligences Pathways to Literacy: Making SMILIES.* Arlington Heights, Illinois: SkyLight Training and Publishing Inc. This handbook helps teachers explore innovative techniques to teaching reading and writing.

Gore, M C. Dowd, John F. (1999). *Taming the Time Stealers. Tricks of the Trade from Organized Teachers.* Thousand Oaks, CA: Corwin Press, Inc. Presents a guide to help teachers manage the multitude of diverse tasks that make up a busy school day.

Nelson, Kristen (1999). Make it a Lesson They'll Never Forget! *Mailbox Teacher, 27* (4), 10-13. Offers suggestions for creating memorable lessons that keep students' attention.

Prabhu, N.S. (1992). The dimensions of the language lesson. *TESOL Quarterly, 26* (2), 224-41. Examines lessons as a curricular event, an implementation of a method, a social event, and an arena of human interaction.

Sanchez, Gaspar. Valcarcel, M Victoria (1999). Science Teachers' Views and Practices in Planning for Teaching. *Journal of Research in Science Teaching, 36* (4), 493-513. Reports on the views and attitudes of secondary science teachers (n=27) toward lesson planning.

Seamon, Mary P. (1999). *Connecting Learning & Technology for Effective Lesson Plan Design.* Paper presented at the Association for Supervision and Curriculum Development Conference, San Francisco, CA. This paper focuses on the design of effective lesson plans using the Internet.

Thornbury, Scott (1999). Lesson Art and Design. *ELT Journal, 53* (1), 4-11. Suggests that teachers should look to the expressive arts for principles and structures for lesson design. Good lessons share features with good films, including plot, theme, rhythm, flow, and a sense of ending.

# CHAPTER 10

# Asking Questions

> "THE acquiring mind, or the inquiring mind. We have a choice."
>
> — UNKNOWN

## INTRODUCTION

Educational fads come and go, but asking and answering questions remains one of the truly fundamental activities of all education. We sometimes forget how powerful the human activity of asking a question and receiving an answer can be. Questions are the essence of communication and of human interaction, sharing, and dialogue. Interestingly enough, like all very common activities, the ability to formulate and ask good questions is often taken for granted.

## CATEGORIZING QUESTIONS

Questions are often categorized according to the thinking processes involved in answering them. The most common categorization scheme involves low and high-level questions. Low-level questions emphasize memory and information recall. Where are the headwaters of the North Saskatchewan River located? Who was the first premier of Alberta? High-level questions go beyond memory and factual information and deal with complex and abstract thinking. What were the reasons for Canada becoming a Confederation? What other alternative courses of action were available to our founding fathers? How would the pursuit of these other alternatives have affected history? These questions are obviously stimulating and challenging. There are no right and wrong answers and they involve more abstractions and points of view.

## ASKING THE RIGHT KINDS OF QUESTIONS

Remember the questions at the end of the chapters of the textbooks you read as a student? Did you like them? Mostly, when we ask this of students, they answer a resounding NO! They hated them, and with good reason.

Sadly, many questions found in student and teacher materials are duds. They seem to be the last thing that textbook writers do. They often ask for narrow responses that encourage students to find only "the facts" in the reading. These kinds of questions are important, but they are also boring, tedious, and encourage students to assume the stance of a passive learner. Second, they never seem to encourage students to "higher-level" activities. The shame is that they never take advantage of what students could (and want to) do if challenged.

So, how should you create questions? Here's a hint: until you become comfortable creating and asking your own "higher-level" questions, use Bloom's Taxonomy to help you think through the kinds of questions you might ask. (We will introduce you to Bloom's Taxonomy later in this chapter.) Bloom's Taxonomy of higher and lower-level activities is not the be-all and the end-all, but it is helpful because it reminds you that there is a wide variety of different questions that can be asked. It also reminds you that certain types of questions encourage certain types of thinking behavior among your students.

There seems to be an educational trend to elevate the importance of higher-order questions and to ignore lower-order questions. Probably, this trend exists because for so many years only lower-order questions seemed to be asked by teachers. The truth is that both higher and lower-order questions are helpful and should be used. Lower-order questions provide an opportunity to bring all students together at a beginning level of understanding.

Lower-order questions are sort of like making sure all your students are on the same page. If your class is like most classes, it has students with a wide variety of abilities. Some students are way ahead and would understand the reading quite easily. Others will not. Answering factual questions helps everyone understand what is being said.

But lower-order questions are not enough. Good questions like good readings should be provocative. Good questions should be interesting and should allow students to explore, to question further, to be critical, to build hypotheses, to evaluate, to make tentative decisions, to support points, and, basically, to think deeply and consider carefully.

Here's another hint about good questions, and it has nothing to do with quality. The number of questions you ask is important. Too few make it seem that the questions are either not important or demand long answers. Too many scare students off. It is also worth keeping in mind that it is good to encourage at least one question per class where students work together in groups.

### WHY ASK QUESTIONS?

There are four basic reasons to ask questions in your classroom. First, you want to keep control and organize your classroom. Second, you want to find out what your students know or what they have learned. Third, you want to direct their learning and point them in the right way so that they can find out what you believe they should know. And fourth, you want to create critical thinking and encourage general intellectual growth.

**Keeping control and organizing the activity of the classroom.** Questions can be both controlling mechanisms and organizing activities in the classroom. Most teachers have learned from their teachers, who have learned from their teachers, some tips about classroom control. The first tip is an implicit understanding that if you put students on the spot they will be quieter. Really, it's not a bad tip. The teacher who uses questions as a management tool is one who looks around while he or she is talking, sees a student who is sleeping, daydreaming, or whispering, and asks that student about what is being discussed in class. The response of the student is usually to attend to the teacher's voice (and question) and stop the offending or off-topic activity. The teacher's question is of secondary importance to the student's response to the question.

Probably every teacher uses this management technique and with good reason. It works. The problem with it is that the question becomes secondary to the effect of the question. This is OK occasionally, but a steady stream of such questioning in a classroom renders the lesson activity impotent and is a focus on negative, rather than positive, behavior.

> **"Every question does not deserve an answer."**
> *- Publilius Syrus*

Questions can also serve as a lesson plan activity. The teacher gives students questions to "do" and the students do the questions. Often questions that structure the activity live in worksheets to be done in class, or as homework, or on lists at the end of textbook chapters. Again, using questions as a lesson plan activity is not a bad thing. Where the activity goes wrong is when it is done all the time. A memorable example was in the movie *Teachers*, where the teacher left sheets of questions for the students to complete. The students came into class, picked up and answered the questions silently, and then turned them in for the teacher to grade later. In the movie, the teacher died in the morning and no one noticed. The class went on all day long with the teacher's body propped in the desk at the back of the room.

**Finding out what your students know or what they have learned.** Questions are the best way to find out whether students have learned what was taught and to what extent they have learned it. This point is especially true if the content of the lesson is factual or conceptual. (Skills are best evaluated through demonstration and replication.)

Here's a simple hint about asking questions: if you want to know an answer, ask a question. Maybe this statement seems to border on the banal; however, we often see teachers excessively worried about whether their students are learning, or what their students know when they come into their classroom, or if a particularly difficult concept or idea has been grasped. Certainly, teachers should have these concerns in mind. Teachers need to know. If they don't act in some diagnostic fashion, they fail to help their students. But often the concern can be easily satisfied by the simple act of asking.

We encourage teachers to be direct (not rude). If you want to know something, ask. Give little quizzes. Give many exams. Ask students to repeat what they have learned in a variety of ways. Seek responses from the class. It not only solves the problem of the need to know; it also makes the class more active and responsive.

**Directing students' learning.** Questions can be used to point students in the right direction. As students respond to questions, they are following a pre-determined path. The activity is really quite simple. Questions at the end of a textbook chapter refer students to the chapter. Questions that must be answered using an atlas help students learn how to use an atlas. As students respond to questions, they react in an unconscious dialogue with you, the teacher. You find out what they know, and they find out what you believe they should know.

The answering of any question is the student's response to a task. By carefully setting the task, you are creating the learning environment in which the student lives. You can also create an effective learning environment by giving students the opportunity to create their own questions. This task, itself, helps students speculate about what is important and what is not. And it helps them move to what they don't know from what they do know. This movement is a key to learning.

**Creating critical thinking.** Probably the most important function of classroom questioning is that it moves students from passivity to activity. And by creating this movement it encourages general intellectual growth. We heard a teacher teasingly call his students "sponges." They sucked up what he said, and when it came to tests they dripped it out a drop at a time onto the paper. He encouraged his students to move away from being consumed with "what do you want" to a position of creating their own knowledge by risking or daring to ask the important questions for themselves.

If you sincerely want to move your students toward critical thinking, the kinds of questions you ask are ultimately important. You must ask questions even you do not know the answer to. It is one kind of learning to find the answers to the factual points that are in the text; the students respond. It is another kind of learning to help students come to the belief that they can and should become responsible for their own learning; the students create.

Our goal for students is to help them learn to see that what they are studying has to do with the reality of their own lives. We want them to understand what's going on in their subject area, how this relates to the world they live in, and how their answers encourage them to take responsibility for what they learn in the course of living their lives. Specifically, we have a political agenda. We believe that students should learn to use what they learn to be active, to be intellectual "doers" and "not hearers only." You may think that answering questions is about learning what's in a chapter, but we don't. We think that there's a lot more to it than just knowing. It's called taking responsibility for what you learn.

> "The imitative student if given a question will answer it. The creative student if given an answer will question it."
>
> *- Edgar Dale*

## CREATING QUESTION TYPOLOGIES

To help accomplish the goals we have for our classes, we use typologies of questions that address the particular needs to which we wish to attend. This may sound like a complex task, but it's really quite simple. Remember, our criticism of questions asked in schools is that they seem to focus exclusively on the recall of knowledge—the lowest level of Bloom's Taxonomy. Focusing on the content is essential, but good questions draw human life into the discussion as well.

The first task in creating a question typology is to consider the goals of your teaching. What do you really want to do? What do you really want your students to learn? As a beginning teacher, we would encourage you to take short notes about your goals. Write down what you want to accomplish. Where do these goals come from? The answer is that they come from two sources: (1) the curricular program of studies you are required to teach in whatever jurisdiction you are teaching, and (2) your own best understandings of the task and importance of education—from what you believe and from the books that you have read as you have prepared to become a teacher.

## TWO TYPES OF QUESTION TYPOLOGIES

Whenever we have written textbooks that students use in schools, we have created a specific organizational pattern that helps teachers and students organize their own questioning. Below, we will highlight two of these patterns. The specific patterns themselves are not cast in stone, but each shows a way that (1) specifically organizes the activities that you want your students to do, and (2) pushes past the simple recall of knowledge.

**Typology One** is based on Bloom's Taxonomy. It is simple and organized in a hierarchy. When you have created a typology, remember that it is not a recipe. It is not to be used 1-2-3-4. That would be insipidly boring. Instead, the typology serves as a reminder of the different types of questions you might use.

When constructing the typology, create the following types of questions:

Question One is a knowledge (remembering) question.
Question Two is a comprehension (understanding) question.
Question Three is an application (transferring) question.
Question Four is an analysis (relating) question.
Question Five is a synthesis (creating) question.
Question Six is an evaluation question.

Remember that questioning is more an art than a technique. There are no perfect questions. At certain times, some questions are better than others. At other times, the same question would be inappropriate. This specific typology was created to help students develop a hierarchy of skills.

How do you know if you have created a question in each category? First, don't worry about specifically fitting into a category. A typology is a reminder, not a set of laws. However, there are key verbs (verbs describe student activities) that will help create a range of good activities for your students. Each question type includes key words that help students focus their activities.

Activities in the question format are distinguished by the following key verbs or activities:

Question One: define, describe, identify;
Question two: summarize, paraphrase;
Question Three: apply, use, employ;
Question Four: relate, distinguish, order, contrast;
Question Five: formulate, compose, produce, compare, predict;
Question Six: weigh, decide, give reasons for.

The activities inherent in these questions are helpful because they focus students on skills-based activities. For example, they encourage the growth of process skills (often called meta-cognitive skills—learning how to learn) which include locating, organizing, and interpreting information (analyzing, synthesizing, and evaluating). They also address communication skills, participation skills (like group work), and attitude objectives. Your job as a teacher is to help your students learn more about the "subject" you are teaching and to become more intellectually mature and able learners as they do so.

**Typology Two** is a simple organizational pattern that can be used in setting assignments or, again, in dealing with information that is found in textual narrative. The highlight of this typology is that it pushes the material learned into the real-world lives of students and asks them to reconcile what they know in life with what they learn in school. We think this is a powerful activity because it is implicitly interesting for students.

This typology has been built using four metaphorical concepts: (1) focusing, (2) layering, (3) extending, and (4) deciding to build a pattern of question asking. To show the different types of questions you might ask, we will use a favorite short story to illustrate the point, Charles Dickens' *A Christmas Carol*.

**Focusing questions** help people find out more about the content being studied. For example: In the story *A Christmas Carol*, Dickens shows that Scrooge met a number of people throughout his life. Who are these people? Why do you think he uses them as examples?

**Layering questions** ask people to go past the content being studied and think of other circumstances that are similar to those in the "story." For example: In the story *A Christmas Carol*, things have changed since this story was told; still, many groups remain in the same difficult situations that Dickens describes. If you were going to retell the story in a modern setting, what groups could you use to make the meaning of the story just as authentic? What groups in your own community (define community broadly) might be in similar situations?

**Extending questions** push past situations in the content right into the students' own lives. They are much more personal than layering questions. For example: In the story *A Christmas Carol*, is there a person or group of people that you might be treating in the same way that Jacob Marley and Scrooge treated Bob Crachet, and thus be "collecting chains"? Briefly, rewrite the story of Ebenezer Scrooge substituting the name of the person or group that you choose into the role of Bob Crachet or Tiny Tim. What meaning does the story have for you? Could it be true?

**Deciding questions** ask students to make decisions, evaluate, and make commitments to act on things they've learned. For example: In the story *A Christmas Carol*, what people do you know who have the same characteristics as Ebenezer Scrooge? Is it possible that you could be the "ghost of Christmas yet to come" and help them see a solution to their problems? What long-haul commitment can you make to someone that would really be a help to them? Are you willing?

## THE USES OF QUESTIONS

Certain aspects of teaching get easier the longer you do them. Questioning is one of these aspects. As you teach, you become more practiced in the art of questioning. More able to see how a particular question gets at what you want. More quick to think on your feet and have good things happen instead of bad things. More able to understand not just how you will ask questions, but how your students will hear them. As a new teacher, your experience asking questions is limited and it is probably wise to write out the important questions you will use.

> **"Schools spend too much time teaching answers and too little on how to question answers."**
> *- Unknown*

Once you have created the questions you will use, there are several ways you can apply them. They can be utilized in formal, written evaluations. They can be used orally. Or they can be used at the end of a chapter or section of text. In any of these uses, the basic ideas are similar.

Briefly, there are a number of things we think you should remember when creating and using questions for your students.

1) If you want to know something, ask a question as directly as possible.
2) Questioning is more an art than a technique. There is no single right way to do it.
3) You will become a better questioner with practice. However, until you do become more practiced, it is probably wise to prepare yourself well for questions.
4) There are many uses for questions. Each of these has a place in your classroom, and to become a better teacher you should know how and when to question.
5) Don't forget the power of questions. They can do more than simply help students recall the facts. Consider what you want questions to do, and then create a typology of questions for yourself that will attend to the needs you believe are most important for your students.

## A SAMPLE READING WITH QUESTIONS

The following story appeared in many newspapers across the country. We have provided it as a sample narrative and followed it with a set of possible questions.

### Sniffy the Rat

*Ideas and beliefs differ among people within society. Even the impending death of a vermin can cause the beliefs of people to come into conflict. Such was the case of Sniffy the Rat.*

*Rick Gibson was a 38-year-old, Vancouver artist. For the sake of art, Gibson planned to kill a rat by dropping a 25-kilogram concrete block on the animal. While no one likes rats, Gibson's plans drew threats from animal lovers about a possible riot. The Vancouver Humane Society said that it would rescue Sniffy from death, by force if necessary. Other calls to save the rat came from as far away as Southern Ontario.*

*Gibson the artist remained unmoved. But Vancouver police were. They were worried that Gibson's exhibit would start a riot. "If Sniffy had a choice between a concrete block crushing him quickly and painlessly, or slowly being swallowed by a snake, I think he'd choose me. The rat was going to die anyway." Gibson bought Sniffy from a pet store that used live rats to feed to its pet snakes.*

*One Vancouver art critic noted that the public reaction was part of Gibson's project. If a society were extremely tolerant and an artist killed a rat on the public square, society would say "So what?" It would be meaningless, and the artist wouldn't be able to do it. As an artist, she continued, Gibson depends on the public reaction.*

*What do you think: does Gibson's art work prove how intolerant our society really is?*

Our sample questions surrounding this narrative are as follows:

1) Particular events might be analyzed in two possible ways: (1) what is happening in a narrow sense (the particular facts of the event) and (2) what is happening in a broad sense (the general meaning of the event). Look at the reading about Gibson and Sniffy the Rat from both the narrow and the broad sense. What do you think was happening?

2) The Case Study doesn't mention what happened to Sniffy the Rat. What do you think happened? Can you find out? (Hint: Sniffy was to be killed on January 6, 1989, in Vancouver.)

3) Whose side would you take in this controversy? Why?

4) What does the controversy show about society? How does what happened with Sniffy the Rat prove that civilized people must learn to tolerate even the strangest behavior?

5) Agree or disagree with the following statement and defend your position: Beliefs about what is acceptable behavior differ in society.

## GUIDELINES FOR ASKING QUESTIONS

We mentioned earlier that good questioning is probably more art than technique. However, there are certain guidelines about questioning that seem to apply in most cases. They are as follows:

1) **Wait-time.** This is the time between asking a question and the student response. Many beginning teachers average only 1.5 seconds wait-time. Students need more time than this, particularly for higher level questions, to process information. Obviously, the more complex the question, the longer the necessary wait-time

2) **Directing.** The recommended strategy is to ask a question first of the whole class and then direct it to the student of your choice.

3) **Redirecting and probing.** If a student response is incorrect or inadequate you should not provide the answer. Redirect the question to another student or probe for a better answer from the same student.

4) **Comment and praising.** We know that honest praise (phony or too much praise can have a detrimental effect) increases motivation. The use of smiles, nods of approval, or brief comments encourage students to be actively involved in answering questions.

## A FINAL WORD

As you read this book, you will also find that it is written from a particular point of view. First, we believe that knowing things is important; and, we have tried to fill the book with helpful information. Second, we have tried to write in a way that is readable. Most of all, we have put the textbook together in a way that stresses the power of teachers to make decisions for themselves. We believe that good teachers are naturally curious. We also believe that teachers are able to understand what is happening in their classes.

Thankfully, the days are gone when teachers hide their goals and objectives from their students. For us, questions are more than a method to find out how much content students know. Instead, questioning represents a belief system about teaching that

> **"He who is afraid of asking is ashamed of learning."**
> *- Danish Proverb*

manifests itself in the way teaching is organized. We also believe that the more students know, learn, think, and act, the more intellectually mature they become. We believe that intellectual maturity is the goal of education.

Asking questions represents an invitation to inquiry. Asking questions organizes the class interaction around a belief in inquiry. Good teachers start with questions to help organize students' thinking and exploration as they read. Good teachers encourage their students to study photographs and ask them to explore what they see. Good teachers use end-of-the-chapter questions to organize specific inquiry strategies. Good teachers use questions to help their students pull together what they have learned. Finally, good teachers help students create their own questions as a way to help them organize their study and what will happen throughout the rest of the educational experience.

We encourage you to set a questioning structure that is both simple and complete. We also encourage you to help students by creating a series of questioning strategies and by following this specific strategy in the chapter summaries, questions, and skill-based activities that you use in your teaching.

## READINGS FOR EXTENSION AND ENRICHMENT

Beck, Terence A. (1998). Are There any Questions? One Teacher's View of Students and their Questions in a Fourth-Grade Classroom. *Teaching & Teacher Education, 14* (8), 871-86. Examines a classroom in which fourth graders' questions dominate the discourse, investigating how the teacher reduced forces that discourage student questions in instruction.

Bloem, Patricia L., Manna, Anthony L. (1999). A Chorus of Questions: Readers Respond to Patricia Polacco. *Reading Teacher, 52* (8), 802-08. Describes how the authors worked with five groups of second and fourth graders using picture books to encourage and prompt the children's questions.

Carr, Derek (1998). The Art of Asking Questions in the Teaching of Science. *School Science Review, 79* (289), 47-60. Describes a science department's evaluation of the way teachers use questions in the teaching of science.

Ciardiello, Angelo V. (1998). Did You Ask a Good Question Today? Alternative Cognitive and Metacognitive Strategies. *Journal of Adolescent & Adult Literacy, 42 (3), 210-19.* Encourages secondary and postsecondary content area teachers to encourage student questioning instruction as a basis for higher level thinking about subject matter.

Elder, Linda. Paul, Richard (1997). Critical Thinking: Crucial Distinctions for Questioning. *Journal of Developmental Education, 21* (2), 34-35. Stresses the importance of questioning as a key element in the art of learning.

Elder, Linda. Paul, Richard. (1998). The Role of Socratic Questioning in Thinking, Teaching, and Learning. *Clearing House, 71* (5), 297-301. Argues that questions are essential to thought, that thinking is driven by questions, and that answers often signal a full stop in thought.

Rodriguez, Idalia, Kies, Dan (1998). Developing Critical Thinking through Probative Questioning. *Reading Improvement, 35* (2), 80-89. Suggests a model to develop critical-thinking processes of students to help them deal with a diverse and technologically advanced society.

Savage, Luise B. (1998). Eliciting Critical Thinking Skills through Questioning. *Clearing House, 71* (5), 291-93. Describes an eight-session workshop that develops teachers' abilities to ask questions that are truly thought-provoking.

Schmidt, Patricia Ruggiano (1999). KWLQ: Inquiry and Literacy Learning in Science. *Reading Teacher, 52* (7), 789-92. Describes how two teachers developed an inquiry learning and teaching approach called KWLQ in which students recorded their prior knowledge, formulated questions, searched for answers, and finally noted more questions for further study.

Torres, Bayardo B. (1998). Learning by Posing Questions. *Biochemical Education, 26* (4), 294-96. Recommends utilizing biochemistry problems to develop students' abilities to clearly identify the relevant questions hidden in problematic situations and to select the information required to solve them.

# CHAPTER 11

# Evaluating Students

*THE system of competitive examinations is a sad necessity. Knowledge is wooed for her dowry, not for her diviner charms.*

**- CHARLES SYNGE CHRISTOPHER BOWEN**

## INTRODUCTION

What is evaluation? Evaluation is a way to find things out. When evaluation takes place in schools, its purpose is to find things out about what is happening in the classroom. Specifically, school evaluation exists so that teachers can find things out about students and about themselves as teachers. The reason for evaluation is simple. You will evaluate because you want to know how your students are doing and how you are doing.

This chapter and the one that follows discuss evaluation. The former focuses on what evaluation means for both teachers and students — why and how teachers evaluate. The latter looks at a special form of evaluation — testing.

## PRINCIPLES OF EVALUATION

Before we talk about the "whats," "whys," and "hows" of evaluation, we believe it is important to put forward some principles of evaluation. If you have read the preceding chapters, you will find that these principles are not new. We have tried to repeat them throughout the book.

**Principle One**: Students should know the criteria to be used for judging good or bad work. The purpose of evaluation is to find things out that you don't know and *not* to manipulate an assessment to prove a point. Good evaluation is not tricky. It is honest. It is straightforward. And it is clear.

Students should know and understand the criteria teachers use to judge what is good or bad, what is correct or incorrect, or what is successful or unsuccessful. The reason? During evaluation, you — the teacher — are doing more than just short-term finding out; you are providing information that tells students what is important and what is unimportant. Some of this information will stay with them for the remainder of their lives. Structuring this information is a task not to be taken lightly.

**Principle Two**: Every student should have an opportunity to succeed at one type of evaluation you, as a teacher, use. This principle is based on the belief that no two students have exactly the same abilities. Some can analyze better than others. Some can build a holistic picture and some are better at focusing on the parts. Some do better on objective exams; some like to write.

The practical point is that if you use only one evaluation tool, you may not be gaining an accurate insight into a student's knowledge and abilities. You may hit the student's strength or you may hit a student's weakness. Either way, what you discover is not a reliable "measure" of the student's ability. Our hint: use a variety of different evaluative tools.

**Principle Three**: Students should receive immediate feedback. One of the biggest complaints students have about teachers is that they hand in a paper, an assignment, or an exam and they don't see it again for weeks. Not only is this practice frustrating but it militates against the students' motivation.

There are only two things that students can think when they turn in work and don't get it back: (1) either the work is unimportant in the eyes of the teacher or (2) the teacher is lazy. Immediate feedback encourages and motivates. In addition, it is unfair for a teacher to demand assignments "on time," and then not return them "in time."

One "pit" that many teachers fall into is giving too many assignments. This makes their own teaching (marking) job next to impossible. Eventually these teachers look stupid because they are unable to turn assignments back to students quickly and as a result lose credibility when placing time demands on students' work. We encourage you to be smart. Never give more assignments than you can possibly and realistically grade. It is always better to give no assignment than to give assignments that are not graded with rigor.

## WHY DO TEACHERS EVALUATE?

Our approach in this book has been to be as honest and straightforward as we can be. We will not change our stance when discussing evaluation. There are many possible reasons to evaluate. Some of these reasons will seem more honorable than others. But even the less than honorable reasons for conducting evaluations are still necessary. For the teacher working in a school situation, there are important reasons for evaluating students. These include:

**Diagnosis.** Teaching is more than presenting facts and concepts from specific subject areas. If students are to learn on their own, which is a sign of intellectual maturity, they must possess the skills of learning — basic skills such as reading and writing, or specific skills such as finding the main points and understanding the difference between fact and opinion. These are skills that enable students to work within the classroom and later on within society as they live their lives. Most elementary school teachers realize that school is more than factual material; many secondary school teachers do not. Students never lose their need to develop the skills of reading, writing, and researching. We will echo the comments of many teachers in the areas of reading and writing when we say, "All teachers are teachers of reading and writing, regardless of the grade level where they teach."

> "As long as learning is connected with earning, as along as certain jobs can only be reached through exams, so long we must take the examination system seriously. If another ladder to employment was contrived, much so-called education would disappear, and no one would be a penny the stupider."
>
> *- E.M. Forster*

One reason that teachers evaluate is to find out whether their students are able to understand the skills that they need in order to learn. Evaluation can diagnose whether students have mastered the skills of learning — things like reading, writing, and arithmetic. Evaluation can also help you know to what extent they have mastered these skills. And if the teacher learns that the students have not learned these skills, a prescribed set of treatments is planned.

Obviously, the task of evaluation isn't always as clinical as formal diagnosis and prescription. Sometimes the teacher diagnoses quickly and intuitively, deciding on the fly whether to go once more through a particular topic or whether to move on. The point of this note is to acknowledge that part of evaluation is the diagnosis of specific or general student skills and the creation of plans to overcome areas of deficiency in those skills.

**Creating marks for a report card**. Creating marks for a report card may not seem like an "honorable" reason to evaluate. Still, it is hard to imagine schools without report cards. Report cards have become a formal and expected way for schools to communicate both with the students and the students' parents. Report cards are more than simple reporting mechanisms. They are the "Ghosts of Christmas Past" and "Ghosts of Christmas Yet-to-Come." They tell about the past and they outline the future. Because many students are not yet self-motivated, report cards are the encouragement some students need. Report cards can also serve as the motivation some parents need to take notice of what's happening in school and involve themselves in their child's education.

Because the report card serves so many different functions, creating grades for the report card is as much an art as it is an accounting. For example, no right-thinking teacher would base the entire report card grade on one evaluative test or quiz. Part of the skill of reporting grades is to make sure there are enough grades to give a broad and reliable picture of what the student has been doing.

Furthermore, report cards are rarely as impersonal and objective as they seem from the outside. In fact, report cards can be one of the most powerful things that happens to students in school — shaping their lives well beyond the classroom. For example, when Parsons was teaching grade seven, the counselor visited his classroom after school for a conversation about one of his students (Julia). Julia was a "free spirit," a pleasant young woman who couldn't remain quiet or stay on task for more than a few minutes. Sometimes she handed work in; sometimes she did not. Consequently, her report cards in all subjects were less than average.

The counselor brought a disturbing message. Report cards were coming out later that week, and if Julia got a bad grade on her report card in Parsons' class her father was going to beat her up. The counselor was sure this wasn't just an idle threat. The teacher, in this case, faced a problem. Julia, by the measure of the account's tape, should have received a low grade. But, should the teacher, knowing what he knew, give Julia the grade she "deserved?" (Note: The result, by the way, was that the teacher created a sort of buy-now-pay-later plan and Julia received a higher grade than she would have. The point of this story is not that teachers should give students grades they don't "deserve," but instead that creating grades for a report card is often a dilemma.)

**Encouraging self-improvement**. Every student in your class will be different. Although most school materials and curricula seem to assume that students are equal in all aspects, they are not. Some are gifted with the comforts of life; some have few comforts. Some are naturally more discerning than others. And some have talents in some areas, but not in others. However, regardless of your students' abilities, all students can learn and improve. Similar to the dated, named pencil marks on grandpa's kitchen wall that show the height changes of all the grand children, students need to know they are progressing and growing in their abilities.

An important event that happens in school is that students create a story about their lives, with them as the main character. But the teacher plays a key role in that story — the storyteller. Some of the chapters in the student's story include "Am I a Success, or Not?" and "What Do Important Others Think of My Worth?" Obviously, there are a variety of storytellers in any child's life; but one of the most important — maybe, even, *the* most important — is the teacher. The teacher is the one person with the vested authority to pronounce a student capable or not capable, smart or stupid, worthy or unworthy. Every report card is a plot in the student's story; every evaluation a sub-plot. Why is evaluation so important to students? Because students use these plots and sub-plots to shape and write the future stories of their lives.

Students often seem caught in the eternal now. It's a function of their age. Maybe it's because young people have a talent for viewing themselves so closely and so harshly. It is sometimes difficult for students to see that they are coming from a past; they are moving forward; they are growing; and they are more able than they once were. It is refreshing for them to pause for a moment and to be shown that, yes, indeed, they were once there and now they are here. Sometimes evaluation can be a cause for little celebrations surrounding the hundreds of little, incremental victories of progress made in school as students learn. Evaluation can show students that they have improved.

> "Examinations are harmless when the examinee is indifferent to the result, but as soon as they matter, they begin to distort his attitude to education and to conceal its purpose. The more depends on them, the worse their effect."
> - *Richard Livingstone*

**Reporting and discussing students with parents.** Over the years, schools have changed. Once they were informal, local, and parent controlled. Schools were places where parents were almost ever-present. Today, they are generally operated at arms length from parents. And sadly and too often, parents seem estranged from their children's education. They don't always know what is going on in the places where their children spend so much of their lives away from home.

One job of evaluation is to create opportunities for messages to be sent from the teacher and the school to the parents and from the parents to the school. The most formal evaluation tool is, as mentioned before, the report card. But, certainly, notes from the teacher to the parents can also be important evaluative opportunities — even if they are informal.

Here's a hint about teaching: only use as much formality as you need to do the job you want to accomplish. The smallest actions of the teacher can be extremely powerful. For example, making and enforcing a rule that your students have to introduce you to their parents if you ever meet outside class helps shape the way your classroom works. Inviting parents to school events or into your class as guest speakers. Sitting with parents at basketball games. Calling them to tell them that their child has done something extremely well. These little actions may seem simple, but they create extremely effective structures for informal evaluations to flow back and forth between parents and teachers. We encourage you to use them.

**Evaluation is used to tell students how much they already know**. Many teachers seem to have a negative, punitive view of evaluation. They use evaluation like a big hammer. Evaluation is only useful, they suggest, if it can be used to bludgeon students into submission. But one positive and useful tool of evaluation is to show students that, yes, they do know something. Much like encouraging self-improvement, some evaluation can be used to show students that they have learned the material well. Success is a powerful encouragement.

## WHAT ARE WE EVALUATING?

When most books write about evaluation, they usually begin with a review of two important concepts — formative and summative evaluation. Simply, formative evaluation is evaluation that leads to on-sight decision-making. Summative evaluation is evaluation that wraps-up and serves as a final grading of what students have learned after the topic or unit has been completed.

For example, formative evaluation happens when a math teacher wants to know if students are able to understand the concept of dividing fractions before they go on to the next topic. Formative evaluation happens when, in one way or another, you stop to ask: "Can my students divide fractions?" To conduct this formative evaluation, you might create a simple evaluation tool that tells you how your students are doing on this one point.

> "Even superficial experience teaches us that the results of an examination are valid only for the day when it is held."
>
> *- Johann Herbart*

An example of summative evaluation, on the other hand, is the final exam given at the end of the year or at the end of a report card period. In this case, summative evaluation serves as a summary of the knowledge students hold at the end of a unit. Formative evaluation is useful for making decisions; summative evaluation is useful for reporting the final grades that a student should receive for a course of study.

We believe that it's good to understand the concepts of formative and summative evaluation. However, we have chosen to talk about evaluation in a slightly different manner. We decided that, as important as formative and summative evaluation are, it would be more helpful to you if we suggested many of the things that you might evaluate as a teacher. We also decided that it might be helpful if we then suggested some of the ways you could evaluate these things. The next section gives a brief suggestion of some of the things you might evaluate.

What should a teacher evaluate? The answer to this question can be answered with another question: How do teachers know when they've been successful? So, how **do** teachers know when they've been successful? The answer is that they set up little evaluations to measure what they have done.

Our answer to the question "What should a teacher evaluate?" is also quite simple. We say, "Teachers should evaluate everything." Of course, not all of these evaluations are formal. Some may be almost unconscious. But the fact is, good teachers are always assessing and figuring out what is going on in their classrooms. Good teachers do this because they feel, and are, responsible for the activities that take place where they live and work — their classroom.

Constant evaluation might seem like an unlikely prospect in teaching, but we believe it holds some merits. First, it suggests that what you ask students to do is important. When our student teachers come back from large blocks of time in the schools, we often have them play students for about 15 minutes of one class. Whenever we ask them to do anything, from handing out paper to working in a small group, one of the most common things they say to mimic students is "Does this count for marks?" If it doesn't count for marks, they suggest, it won't get done. Students expect evaluation.

A second reason for evaluating often is that, as mentioned before, you need to create much "evidence" for a report card grade. More evaluations give you a better sense and a more accurate perception of what your students are doing.

A third reason for evaluating often is that evaluation is like the salt that gives the work that students do a seasoning. Evaluating classroom activity adds a touch of seriousness to what is going on in the classroom. When students know that work is being evaluated, they tend to take school a bit more seriously. For some students, taking school more seriously is good; but we have also seen students who — believe it or not — need to take school less seriously.

## DILEMMAS OF CONSTANT EVALUATION

Teachers face at least two potential problems in evaluation. The first is that students equate evaluation with tests. If they don't have a test, they don't know that they are being evaluated. To many students, an informal evaluation is simply not an evaluation at all. Furthermore, students don't always realize what you as a teacher are doing with evaluation until, in many cases, years later.

The second potential problem is that constant evaluation can become a vicious cycle. Ultimately, the goal of education is to encourage intellectual maturity. One sign of intellectual maturity is the ability to be self-motivated, not simply motivated by external forces — things like tests. The dilemma is this: if students expect all their work and assignments to be evaluated, to be "marked," they may come to depend more strongly on these marks as encouragement for their learning.

The resulting situation can be tricky. As a teacher, you want to encourage self-motivation and not simply the response to external stimuli. Yet, you want your students to know that the work they do is not trivial. The answer is that students need to be "re-programmed." Eventually, they need to learn to be smart about what is happening in school and how what is happening there affects their lives after school. Notice the term "eventually." The move from external motivation — things such as tests and other evaluations — to internal motivation is a slow but important process

Often, teachers use only exam-like structures to evaluate students' progress and work. However, there are a number of other possiblities. These other ways to evaluate include student presentations, physical skills that students display, writing assignments, thinking processes, cooperative skills, and any host of other activities. In short, whatever you decide is an important function of your classroom can, and probably should, be evaluated.

Basically, however, we believe that there are four reasons to evaluate. Each of these reasons can be broken down and thought of as an "area" of evaluation. While there are many ways to break evaluation down to study it, we have chosen four basic areas. Similar to all sets of categories, ours are artificial. We created them to suggest that the task of assessment can be divided into useful areas. For example, critics may say that our category 3 and our category 4 are both high level areas. They are probably correct. However, we needed to make a distinction to suggest variety. Remember, other categories are probably just as useful as ours. We happen to like these because, basically, they are ours.

The areas of evaluation we have chosen to consider are: (1) Assessing knowledge and comprehension, (2) Assessing the application of skills, (3) Assessing higher level thinking skills (including analysis and synthesis), and (4) Assessing critical thinking.

## HOW ARE WE EVALUATING?

There are many possible ways to evaluate. Some of these ways include anecdotal records, checklists and charts, conferences, portfolios, tests and quizzes, and evaluations of students' reading, writing, and mathematical skills. Evaluation may be holistic, analytic, primary trait, self-evaluation, etc. The point here is that evaluation is more than a test. There are many ways to evaluate.

To help you get a sense of how you might evaluate your students' work, we will offer some suggestions in the four areas of evaluation we have set out. These suggestions are not comprehensive. Instead, they are offered as examples of the sorts of non-testing activities teachers may use to evaluate. Please note that there are many other evaluation techniques. We encourage you to be very creative. If you have an idea, try it. If it doesn't work, forget it and try something else. We know this from our own experience: sometimes the best evaluation ideas come from crazy thoughts that hit you when you are stuck in traffic. Don't forget these crazy thoughts. Sometimes they are not as crazy as you might think.

> "The examination system, and the fact that instruction is treated mainly as training for livelihood, leads the young to regard knowledge from a purely utilitarian point of view, as the road to money, not as the gateway to wisdom."
>
> *- Bertrand Russell*

**Assessing knowledge and comprehension.**The task of assessing knowledge and comprehension is to find out how much your students know. Many teachers rely solely on quizzes and tests; however, here are some other ideas you might use to assess knowledge and comprehension.

1. Student-created Review Games (e.g., jeopardy, word search, crossword puzzles): The purpose of student-created games is to have students do the teacher's work. There are at least two reasons why having students do the work can be helpful. First, it saves the teacher time. Second, the old saying is that one never learns a thing so well as when one is preparing to teach it. As students do the work of the teacher, they learn more. Why? Because they are active instead of passive. And because they are beginning to "think like the teacher." They are breaking things down and putting them back together — analyzing and synthesizing. Students can and should be involved in creating the puzzles and games themselves. They can be evaluated by their involvement and the quality of the work they complete.

2. Writing Rap Songs: The purpose of having students write "Rap" music is to provide a format where they can collect and present information to one another. The rap music format is almost perfect because

the chorus tends to repeat the important concepts and ideas while the verses outline the specific facts. One of the most positive aspects of asking students to put together a rap song is that, to do so, they must go over the material repeatedly to write the lyrics. A second positive aspect is that most students love to perform. (Note: we have used this idea successfully from elementary schools to university courses.) Once students have put their lyrics and music together, they can perform their song — either on tape or live. And because the performances highlight the course content, as other students listen — you may even want to tape the presentations — they are learning.

**Assessing the application of skills.** The aplication of skills can be evaluated in a number of ways. We have included a few for your consideration.

1. Creating Quality Presentations: There is a difference between presentations that are simply acceptable and first-class presentations. Sometimes something looks very good; sometimes something is very good. Teachers can spend time discussing and creating the criteria for evaluation. Then, they can ask their students to complete the presentation.

We like presentations for another reason. Presentations allow the teacher to see students in a different light. In the typical, daily activities of school, students can sit still and wait for the teacher to do all the work. But a presentation changes the position of the student. When presentations happen, students stand and teachers sit. Frankly, we believe that students learn more when they are active than when they are still.

2. Completing a Job Application for a Historical or Literary Character: If you want students to come to understand the lives of the people they are studying in your class, whether these people are historical or even literary, you might ask them some multiple choice, true or false, or matching questions on an exam. Maybe the more typical way would be to ask your students to write a descriptive paragraph about the people or characters. These are useful ways to evaluate what they know.

However, another way to evaluate their knowledge might be to find or create a job application form for them to fill out about the person or character. In filling out any job application form, the person filling out the form must provide information like height and weight, address, background, previous employment, a list of references, and reasons why the applicant would be good at the particular job. This information is also instructive about the person or character. An added benefit is that when the assignment is completed and students review the work, they also gain some insight into how they might better fill out a job application of their own.

**Assessing higher level thinking skills.** These higher level thinking skills include analysis and synthesis.

1. Portfolios: Basically, a student portfolio is a purposeful collection of a student's work. What makes this collection different from other evaluation types is that the collection is usually created as a result of the student's personal assessment of his or her best work. It is put together to show effort, progress, and growth to the teacher, to other students, to parents, and to others.

A portfolio is evaluated by demonstrating student growth. It is an assessment of higher level thinking skills because it includes the student's analysis of work and the synthesis of putting this work together into a collection. Any useful portfolio must include student participation in the selection of the content of the portfolio, an outline of the criteria for making selections for the portfolio, the criteria used for judging the quality of the work in the portfolio, and evidence that the student has thought about and can give reasons for placing material in the portfolio.

> "No educational system is possible unless every question directly asked of a pupil at any examination is either framed or modified by the actual teacher of that pupil in that subject."
> *- Alfred North Whithead*

2. Writing Newspapers or Newspaper Articles: A simple way of assessing higher level thinking skills such as analysis and synthesis is to ask students to create an alternative format for organizing the content they are studying. One alternative format is the newspaper.

For example, if students are studying Newtonian physics in science, or Brazil in social studies, or *Hamlet* in language arts, or fractions in math, they could pull what they know about the topic together into a newspaper format. They could write articles for the paper in which each student presents a different aspect of the content. In writing the article, they could create characters, add events, and even create ads or cartoons. Without stretching the format much, one could even do an Ann Landers' column about the use of fractions. In creating this newspaper, higher level thinking skills would naturally be addressed.

**Assessing critical thinking**. Critical thinking can be evaluated in a number of ways. We have included a few for your consideration.

1. Students Decide Goals: Generally, teachers decide what is important in the classroom and how the classroom should be run. There's nothing wrong with these decisions: making decisions is one of the primary tasks of the teacher. However, simply because deciding, organizing, and goal-setting are necessary tasks of the teacher doesn't mean that the teacher **always** has to be the primary "decider," organizer, and goal-setter of the classroom.

Sometimes, it is good for students to set their own goals and to work to meet them. Setting goals requires both creative and critical thought. It also requires a sense of evaluation of what is important and what is not. It requires time management, and it requires organizing a way to assess whether goals have been met at the end of the work.

2. Students Becoming the Teacher: As mentioned earlier, there is an old saying among teachers that "You never learn so much as when you prepare to teach." We believe that this saying is true. But what also makes the saying important for teachers is that it suggests a possible teaching strategy that can help improve students' critical thinking. Let them become teachers for a while.

In preparing to teach the class, and by this teaching we mean more than simply a short presentation, students in groups will plan an entire class period, will organize and create materials, will work on directions to their peers, will teach the content or skills, and will evaluate what their peers have learned. During the time the students are acting as teachers, the teacher will become a student — certainly a more relaxing position in the classroom.

## ALTERNATIVE METHODS OF EVALUATION

The alternatives to traditional testing in evaluation are limited only by your imagination. We will briefly explore the use of journals, conferences, and presentations as evaluation methods in the discussion to follow. Do you have other ideas?

**Journal writing.** Thoughts, no matter how terrific, can be fleeting. It's difficult for anyone to remember and make sense of all the thoughts that flit through a brain in a day. Students, in particular, need a place to gather their thoughts and a time to consider their learning.

Journals, or learning logs, are a valid way of giving students a time and a place to record their thinking, to question their own thoughts and the thoughts of others, to extend their ideas and to make connections with the ideas of other people. Journals also encourage students to foster good habits — habits like thinking about their reading, writing about their ideas, taking risks. Journals are safe places to risk asking questions, to make judgments, and to outline visions. They're a good place to begin to make meaningful conversation.

Journals can take various formats. Some of these formats include reader response notebooks, dialogue journals, and learning logs. They can allow students to reread their earlier thoughts and view their own progress or misunderstandings. Journals encourage connections and extend thinking, allowing for the creation of new ideas that may span more than one subject area. They may provide the kernel of an idea for an extended project or activity.

Using journal writing as a method of assessment is not difficult. However, if you are to use it successfully with your students, it is important to realize that journal writing happens quickly and that the meaning of the words is usually more important than the grammar and punctuation. While it is important for teachers to instruct their students so that they might become more polished writers, to demand accuracy to the exclusion of meaning holds the potential of slowing down, or even putting a halt to, the writing process.

**Conferencing.** One of the most efficient and direct ways to gain information about students' understandings and progress is to ask them to talk about it with you. It may be time-consuming for you to individually conference with each student, but these conferences can provide valuable information about the student and even about you as a teacher. If there is one thing to understand about students as people it is that they are, in fact, people. You may not see these people in the panorama of your class, because individuals can melt into students. But, as you speak with your students, you will come to know them better and better.

> "I *always* get seventy-eight. No more, no less. It's nerve wrack-ing. I'd almost rather flunk once in a while."
>
> *- Ruth Gordon*

Conferences can be brief and informal. They can take place on the fly, as you walk around your class checking on individual student work. Or conferences may be structured in a more formal way. Informal conferences are easier to manage time-wise. Still, formal conferences have the advantage of having a direct focus; and our experience is that students usually appreciate directness. This direct focus can allow for thoughtful input on the part of the students.

The questions you ask students in a conference can provide information about students' work from their own points of view. The focus questions you write as you prepare for these conferences provide a basis from which you might begin to discuss the students' work, either work in progress or work that is completed. In formal conferences about completed work, students can also have input about the future directions of their work (setting goals, for example) and into the grading process that you have set out. We have found that conversations with students about the system of grading we use are always helpful. We also have gained insight and instruction from students and, we believe, have used students' input to construct grading ideas that are more fair and understandable to our students.

Besides teacher and student conferences, peer conferences (student with student) can be used. Students can discuss each others' work using questions provided by the teachers or questions decided by large group class discussion. When students gain the ability to create their own questions and comments, you will know that learning has taken place. Working with another student partner also has the advantage of helping each student improve his or her work. Peer conferencing benefits both partners by helping them establish criteria for their work and by helping them become more critical readers and listeners.

**Student Presentations**. There are a variety of types of presentations that students might do. We have seen a variety of successful ideas used by teachers. Some include role-playing Shakespeare, creating historical drama, news reports, puppet shows, Oprah Winfrey Shows, writing scripts, doing newscasts, conducting man and woman on the street interviews, using audio-tapes for reading plays, writing rap songs to review historical events, and using final projects rather than exams. We also encourage the use of technology, like videos, so that students can self-evaluate their work.

By student presentations, we do not mean finding a current events newspaper article and reading it to an audience of yawning friends. These boring sorts of activities (if they are active at all) are not worth the time they take to complete. By student presentations, we mean first-class, well-worked-out presentations. We have seen students work together creatively and rigorously, getting ready to present their own idea for a new radio station to the Canadian Radio and Television Corporation (CRTC). We have seen them learn about how federal decisions are made, and how to put together a first-class proposal to a governmental organization, and how to interact with others with tolerance and without rudeness.

> "To those who know, a written examination is far from being a true criterion of capacity. It demands too much of memory, imitativeness, and the insidious willingness to absorb other people's ideas. Parrots and crows would do admirably in examinations. Indeed the colleges are full of them."
>
> *- Stephen Leacock*

One of the most interesting things about student presentations is that you can often come to see a different side to students as they present. As teachers, we have often asked ourselves after watching a presentation, either live or on tape, where some of these people have been hiding. Certainly, we have never seen this creative, and often "wild and crazy," side to our students' personalities. The year is almost over, and we still see facets of our students that we have missed. We believe that as teachers we do not constrain and we hope that we did not stifle; still, the presentation format allows us to see and to assess a different side of our students — a side we have come to appreciate.

## A FINAL WORD

Evaluation is more than tests and quizzes. It provides an opportunity to see our students in a variety of different and important ways; and if we do it well, it allows us to help our students grow and mature. We encourage you to try a variety of different ideas for assessment. In this chapter, we have only provided a few ideas. Certainly, we have not covered the issue.

How you evaluate is for you to work out as you teach. We encourage you to actively think about what you do as teachers and to choose evaluation and assessment activities that bring out the best in your students. We also believe that your attitude about assessment and evaluation is even more important than the methods you use. We encourage you to try many ideas. You will find some that work and some that don't. If you do find things that work, we encourage you to go one extra step. Share what you have learned with another teacher. In this way, you can learn to assess your own work — the sign of a maturing professional.

## READINGS FOR EXTENSION AND ENRICHMENT

Airasian, Peter W. (1997). *Classroom Assessment* (3rd ed.). New York: McGraw Hill. Book shows how assessment principles apply to the full range of teacher decision making, and not just the formal evaluation of student learning.

Airasian, Peter W. Jones, Ann M. (1993). The Teacher as Applied Measurer: Realities of Classroom Measurement and Assessment. *Applied Measurement in Education, 6* (3), 241-54. Explores how informal assessment is used to inform daily classroom decisions, and how these decisions spill over into formal measurement and assessment.

Barrow, Dorian A. (1993-94). The Use of Portfolios to Assess Student Learning. *Journal of College Science Teaching, 22* (3), 148-53. Describes how one teacher and 46 general chemistry students used portfolios as part of the evaluative process.

Bateson, David (1994). Psychometric and Philosophic Problems in "Authentic" Assessment: Performance Tasks and Portfolios. *Alberta Journal of Educational Research, 40* (2), 233-45. Suggests that high standards of reliability and validity are essential in the use of "authentic" methods.

Cooper, Charles R, Ed. Odell, Lee, Ed. (1999). *Evaluating Writing: The Role of Teachers' Knowledge about Text, Learning, and Culture.* Urbana, IL: National Council of Teachers of English. Intended to guide writing teachers through the complexities of evaluation, the essays in this collection represent a variety of approaches to evaluation.

Fenwick, Tara J., Parsons, Jim (1999). Using Dynamic Assessment in the Social Studies Classroom. *Canadian Social Studies, 34* (1), 153-155. Explores how teachers can evaluate the development of various dynamic skills in social studies.

Elliott, Stephen N. (1995). *Creating Meaningful Performance Assessments.* ERIC Digest No. E531. (Report No. EDO-EC-94-2). Reston, VA:   ERIC Clearinghouse on Disabilities and Gifted Children. (ERIC Document Reproduction Service No. ED 381 985). This digest offers principles of performance assessment as an alternative to norm-referenced tests.

Lyman, Howard B. (1998). *Test Scores and What They Mean* (6th ed.). Needham Heights: Allyn & Bacon. Explores the practical use and interpretation of test scores.

# CHAPTER 12

# Testing Students

"EXAMINATIONS are formidable, even to the best prepared, for the greatest fool may ask more than the wisest man can answer."

**- CHARLES CALEB COLTON**

## INTRODUCTION

This statement may be shocking, but we love evaluation. What may be even more shocking is that students love being evaluated. The only time they don't appreciate being evaluated is if they are doing poorly. So the task is simple: before evaluating students make sure they will do well when evaluated.

You may wonder why we are so enamored with evaluation. We encourage you to make huge, comprehensive exams, to review vocabulary and test it, to send tests home, and evaluate whenever possible. Quite simply, our experience teaching in both junior and senior high schools has taught us the power of having a variety and large number of evaluations (making many grades).

This chapter is about one special part of evaluation — testing. Creating and writing tests can be a learning experience for both teachers and students. As teachers, whenever we create test questions, we must decide what material is valuable and what material we want students to remember.

Regardless of subject matter, students' knowledge and understandings can be tested in a variety of ways. It is possible, for example, to use either subjective or objective tests in mathematics, or science, or social studies, or language arts. But, just because a variety of tests are possible, doesn't make all testing ideas equal. The proper choice of test or examination format can best be made only after we have carefully considered what aspects of students' knowledge we want to evaluate. Sometimes short answer and multiple choice approaches work best; at other times more subjective formats such as essay are more effective.

This chapter will suggest a variety of ideas; however, it is up to you to make the right choice. Ultimately, it is not what we say that matters; it's what you say. All we can do is provide you with some choices. You must decide.

Here are some of the benefits of exams:

1) They let the students know where they are grade-wise.
2) They encourage students to do their best.
3) If students start to be successful in little things, we have found they will gain more success in big things.
4) Parents will know where their kids stand (what they are studying and how they are doing).
5) When students do well, they get to posture their good grades to their parents, or others who care.
6) Constant evaluation keeps students on task.
7) Constant evaluation helps students get better grades. When this happens, the class loses one of the reasons for conflict between teacher and students.
8) The teacher and the students can work cooperatively to "beat the exam." The task becomes one of mutual goals. And when goals are accomplished, the team can take credit. In this way, evaluation has the potential to turn the natural teacher versus student class setting into an environment of teamwork and cooperation.
9) Once it is clear that the content to be covered has been mastered, the class is more open for other enrichment activities.
10) Having a large number of evaluations allows the teacher to justify grades—especially good grades—without many hassles from administration.
11) Smaller quizzes can be placed in students' notebooks and used as study guides for larger, comprehensive exams (which, after all, basically review the shorter quizzes).
12) Because different students have different abilities, a large number and variety of evaluations allow some students to succeed on one type of evaluation while they may find others more difficult.

(Often in a class with few evaluations, the odds are stacked and biased against some students—no matter how hard they work—because they do not have the skills to succeed.)

## QUICK QUIZZES

When we use the term 'quick quiz', we mean a short quiz given on a smaller amount of material. The basic idea of a quick quiz is to test all the important material within a section, not to be selective. (If there is to be selection, that might come in the comprehensive examination. Our personal encouragement to teachers is to make their comprehensive exams really comprehensive. We say: TEST EVERYTHING.)

We encourage teachers to give quick quizzes (not necessarily pop or unannounced quizzes) for every chapter they use in a textbook. We also encourage teachers to use a variety of different quick quizzes. The only real difference between review activities and the quick quizzes is that the quick quizzes are done without an open book. Again, our encouragement is to save all the work that you complete for any unit. It will be helpful in the years to come, and for making trades with other teachers.

## WHY USE FINAL EXAMS?

We encourage teachers to use comprehensive exams. Exams give teachers a real idea of how their students are doing. (This is not news.) Second, through the process of creating a comprehensive exam, teachers make decisions about what content is worth knowing. A comprehensive exam serves as a guide for designing teaching plans. Third, a comprehensive exam helps students focus on what they are doing in class. If students know that a comprehensive exam waits for them sometime soon, most will attend to the activities of the classroom in a more rigorous manner. Fourth, we found that a comprehensive exam, when students did well, provided a real sense of success and accomplishment. Furthermore, the longer and harder the comprehensive exam, the more students felt they

> **"No one knows what he can do until he tries."**
> *- Publilius Syrus*

accomplished **when** (not if!) they completed it successfully. [One of our main tasks as teachers is helping students do well on their exams. This places us on the side of the students and not in a conflict situation with them. Our job is to teach.] Fifth, a teacher can send the completed and graded exam home with students for their parent to sign and return. Teachers in our past did this, but for different reasons than we do it. We're confident our teachers wanted to show our parents how terrible we were and wanted to encourage them to frighten us into working harder. But our goal is more gentle and probably more devious. We want to show-off to parents. First, we want them to know that we are teaching vast amounts of content. Second, we want them to know that their kids are being extremely successful on the very difficult and comprehensive exams we are making.

As we have stated in a number of other places in this book (we feel it is worth repeating), we believe there is a "success cycle" at work in schools. If kids experience a little success, they will find out it feels good. We believe this feeling will encourage them to work just a little harder to have more success—just because they like the idea of feeling good.

In our experience, we found that, generally, the theory worked. Over our teaching careers, we have had a large number of parents tell us how surprised and pleased they were that their kids were learning so much. Of course, we humbly took credit for every success the students had. When students did well we were able to give them good marks on their report cards. The kids liked this; their parents liked this; and, when the administration of our schools complained about the marks (inferring that we were grading too easy), we showed them the comprehensive exams and encouraged them to take them. What could they do?

These are some of the reasons we have included suggestions about how to use comprehensive exams. Later in this chapter, we have provided a variety of evaluation types. If you use ideas like you find here, we feel you will come to know how your students are stacking up against your desire to have them master the knowledge.

As we have mentioned, we believe that giving students a large final exam does not punish them for their lack of knowledge, but allows them to show how much they have learned. We also believe that teachers should review and review (in the most enjoyable ways possible) the material they consider most important and prepare their students so well for the exam that anyone who pays attention in class will do well.

We offer these suggestions both as an ethical way to teach (it does not prejudice slow learners like most typical systems) and as a practical way to work—the class responds cooperatively. Our experience has been that when students take "the biggest test they have ever taken" and do very well, they increase not only their self-esteem but also their willingness to work harder the next time. We believe that good teaching and good learning go hand-in-hand and that students should have the chance to earn good grades.

We encourage you, in every unit you teach, to design a large exam of your own choosing as a final review of students' knowledge. To do this you might choose from the questions at the end of the chapters, from the review exercises and activities placed in the teachers' guides you use, and from the quick quizzes you design.

## OBJECTIVE VERSUS SUBJECTIVE EXAMS

Should I make an objective (short answer) or a subjective (essay) exam? is a common question from beginning teachers. Our answer is that each type of exam has its good and bad points. An objective test, if students have reviewed the material well and are not thrown off by the form (sometimes teachers can make the form of an objective exam so difficult that even students who know the material cannot answer the exam correctly), is generally easier for all students. Essay exams tend to favor those students who are smarter and have better writing skills.

For teachers, making either essay or shorter-answer exams tends to be an equal amount of work. The question is when you want to do the work? Objective exams are front-heavy. They take much time up front to develop and are relatively easy to grade. The good point is that you can save the exam (or question pool if you have a computer) from one year to the next and cut down on your work the next year. An essay exam is simple to make up, but takes countless hours to grade. And it doesn't get easier to grade year after year. You expend the same effort.

The level of your students makes a difference as well. Junior high students must be able to put their thoughts into words, but they are also working harder setting a basic core of understandings. Presumably, senior high students are learning to rely more on their own ability to decide and to justify their decisions. The difference is not as great as most people believe; however, it does exist and should be considered.

## TYPES OF QUESTIONS FOR OBJECTIVE TESTS

There are different kinds of questions that might be used in a final, comprehensive exam. Each has its good and bad points. Below, some of these are outlined. The good and bad points of each are also briefly described.

**Fill-in-the-blanks** questions provide a sentence where students must know and fill in the appropriate word that completes the sentence. Because the word is not provided, they make it difficult for students to guess. They are also good because they allow students to answer the question within the context of a larger sentence.

> **"There's dignity in suffering— Nobility in pain— But failure is a salted wound that burns and burns again."**
> *- Margaret Eldredge Howell*

Students who have a difficult time reading and spelling can have trouble with fill-in questions and, if a teacher takes off marks for spelling, students with poor language skills can have an even rougher time. One way to make the questions easier and provide spelling and answer clues is to provide a word pool below the questions from which students can choose the correct answers. This move, however, changes the questions from fill-ins into matching.

Fill-in questions are easy to create. However, they should be used with the most important information in the unit. If they are used with trivial information, students may have too tough a time. A sample follows.

1. The _____ _____ began in England in the late 1700's when people started to invent machinery to do their work.

Answer: Industrial Revolution

**Multiple-choice** questions usually provide a stem with a number of alternatives from which a student might choose. The questions might be very easy (a simple definition); more difficult (where more than one answer is correct and students have to choose an alternative that includes more than one choice—(i.e., both a and c are correct); or very difficult, where students must infer a great deal from the text. Easy and more difficult examples follow.

1. (Easy) The year that World War II ended was
   a. 1862
   b. 1945
   c. 1965
   d. 1988
2. (More difficult) Which of the following helped the Japanese people gain a stronger feeling of nationalism?
   a. Japan's isolation from the rest of the world.
   b. the success of Japanese sports industries
   c. the need to sacrifice personal pleasure to industrialize
   d. a and c
   e. all of the above
   f. none of the above
3. (Difficult) Which of the following changes in family relation- ships are brought about by the media? (Below the question, sup- port any answers you choose.)
   a. Families become more isolated.
   b. Families stay at home less.
   c. Families become less friendly.
   d. Children live with their families longer.
   e. Children become more difficult for their parents to handle.

Multiple-choice questions are good questions because they corre- late highly to a student's knowledge. They allow for guessing, but are not as biased against students with poor language skills.

**True-or-false** questions ask students to read a statement and tell whether that statement is either true or false. If students know the information, distinguishing between a true and a false statement is usually easy. If the student does not know the information, the result is a crapshoot. However, the student has, theoretically, a 50-50 chance in this crap shoot. Often teachers make true-or-false questions more difficult by having students tell why false statements are false.

True-or-false questions encourage students to read questions carefully. Often students can be careless. They see two aspects of a question and jump to a conclusion. For example: In 1853, Commodore Matthew Perry became the first person from the Western world to fly into the airport at Tokyo. In this question, a careless student would see both Matthew Perry and 1853 and miss the fact that he sailed into the harbor and did not fly into the airport.

True-or-False questions are easy to construct and quick to grade. Our encouragement is to discourage cheating by asking students to write the entire word (True or False) rather than put T or F in the space provided. Examples follow.

_____1. Technology is an invention of the twentieth century.

_____2. Our work helps define who we are.

_____3. Within the next fifty years, most Canadians will live to see the end of technology.

**Matching questions** work well for people, dates and events, and vocabulary terms and definitions. They usually have little context and are quick evaluations of important nouns. We like matching because a teacher can cover all the important vocabulary terms and grade the questions quickly.

Three hints: (1) Make matching in sections (all on the same page) and no more than 25 terms in a section. More than this can confuse the students; (2) You can discourage a situation where the last few matches are freebies by adding

> **"Learning is discovering that something is possible."**
> *- Fritz Peris*

extra choices to the list of possible definitions; (3) Order each line from left to right so that the space is first, the definition is second, and the letter and term to be matched are on the far right. It makes the questions much easier to grade with a key; (4) make sure that the words and choices are mixed up. An example follows.

___1. Outer edge of kidney     a. Bladder

___2. Urine is stored here     b. Renal vein

___3. Blood vessel leaving kidney     c. Renal cortex

**Short-answer questions** can vary from having students write objective definitions to having them subjectively justify or support points from an argument. They give students a structure for answering, but allow them more freedom in their answers. Short-answer questions are best used for those concepts that are difficult to place in a shorter form or those times when a teacher wants to minimize guessing by students.

They are relatively easy to grade and to design. They offer teachers an opportunity to judge a student's ability to reason or to synthesize information. They encourage students to offer more complete answers. Samples follow of three types of short-answer questions: structured answer, definition and sentences, and synthesis.

**Structured answer sample.** Directions: Identify the following. In your answers, provide information that would (1) suggest that you know what or who these people or groups are and (2) why these groups might be considered important (i.e., what contributions they have made to human life).

1. Rick Hansen
2. Greenpeace
3. CIDA
4. Women's Institutes
5. CAN-MATE

**Definitions and sentences sample.** Directions: Define the following terms. After your definition, write a sentence that uses the term you have defined in a real-life context. (Hint: It's not acceptable for this activity to write a sentence that is a re-definition of the term.)

1. saturated
2. global
3. anabolic steroid
4. biodegradable
5. non-sectarian

**Synthesis sample.** Directions: The chapter you have just finished focuses on how technology can work to improve life for Canadians. In each of the following five areas, give one way that technology can improve life for Canadians.

1. the Great Lakes
2. forest management
3. farming
4. the environment
5. the future

## USE CLEAR DIRECTIONS

Test directions are often taken for granted by teachers who are quite test-wise. It should not be assumed however that students are nearly as test-wise as teachers. For example, a teacher might write a question like "Should the federal government support dictatorships in the Middle East?" fully intending for students to address the question "Why?" But unless the teacher adds the question

> **"If ignorance is bliss, why aren't more people happy?"**
> - *Unknown*

"Why?" to the end of the first question, it is not reasonable to assume that students should or will address the "Why?" part of the question.

At the same time, good directions help guide students' time through a test. For example, note the difference between the following directions.

**Question 1:**  Why has Western influence been important to the growth of Japan?

**Question 2:**  In four sentences, suggest reasons why Western influence has been important to the growth of Japan.

Directions can encourage students to attend to certain points in the exam. For example, "Read the following statements. If the statement is true, write true in the space to the left of the question number. If it is false, write false in the space to the left of the question number. If the statement is false, give a one-sentence reason why it is false. Be careful. There are some 'trick questions.'

## TESTING THE TEST

No teacher should ever give an exam without taking it first. Better yet, ask a teacher friend to take it. Teachers can become "store blind." They can get so close to the exam that they can't see the problems with it. It is much easier to correct a confusing question before the exam than to deal with the impact of the confusion later. Don't assume your first attempt at a test is perfect. Essay questions, especially, are prone to problems, and teachers should exhibit care. If you cannot think of at least one arguable thesis statement off the top of your head chances are it may not be a good question.

## MAKE OBJECTIVE TESTS EASY TO GRADE

With just a little care, short-answer exams can be made much easier to grade. Before you give any exam, imagine how you will grade it. (Where will you sit? What will you do? What do you want to guard against?)

a) For example, in multiple choice, one way to guard against cheating is to ask students to circle the number/letter in the choices and put the number/letter in the space to the left.

b) One way to make exams easier to grade is to always place the space for the number/letter to the left of the paper if you are right-handed and the staple in the top left. (If you are left-handed, place the spaces on the right of the paper and the staple in the top right.)

## CONSTRUCTING ESSAY TEST ITEMS

We have provided some examples of essay test items. Reviewing the question typologies outlined in the previous chapter should help in the design of essay questions.

Short-answer fact-based essay questions:
  1. Define the following terms:
     a. product
     b. interdependent
Inference "thought" questions:
     a. Name one advantage and one disadvantage of the Walkman Personal Stereo System. Give an example for both the advantage and disadvantage.
     b. How has the automobile affected the way humans interact with each other? Give three examples.
Remembering-the-facts questions:
     a. Outline how technology has changed one of the primary industries in Canada.
     b. Give a short overview of how and when Canadian industrialization took place.
     c. Give two examples of how technology has had adverse effects on the food chain.
Personal-opinion essay questions:
     a. Define change. In your definition make sure to give examples of change.
     b. Define progress. In your definition, make sure to give examples of progress. You might want to show how your own definition of progress might differ from the definitions of other people.
     c. What are three of the most important choices you will have to make in the future? For each choice you list, note why it is important to you.

## TEST ADMINISTRATION

### Preparing to give the test

  1) Be sure that all students are prepared physically. Make sure they have all the necessary materials with them (pencils, pens, erasers, rulers, reference materials, etc.).
  2) Be sure that all students are comfortable. Each student should have enough room so as not to be cramped. Have them remove all unnecessary books and papers from their desks.
  3) Before beginning, specify how students should ask questions. It is usually best if students do not disrupt others by asking questions aloud from their seats.

### Giving the test

  1) It is useful to read the test instructions aloud before beginning the test. Allow time for questions at this point.
  2) You should be available to answer student questions during the test.

3) Avoid making disturbing noises such as rattling papers, answering questions in a loud voice, or walking unnecessarily during the test.

4) To end the test in an organized fashion, you should take up all remaining papers when time is called. A brief warning such as, "You have two minutes left and then you must stop writing." is helpful. This allows your students to finish the thought they are working on.

**Test scoring**

1) No matter if the test is objective or subjective, your scoring should always be as objective as possible. Most beginning teachers have a tendency to equalize scores by subconsciously being overcritical and deducting marks from good responses and accepting poor responses from poorer papers.

2) Make a key for scoring the test. The key should provide a guideline for accepting and rejecting answers.

3) If a large number of students miss a relatively easy question, be suspicious of the question. Perhaps the wording was misleading or confusing. In any case, the question may have to be eliminated.

4) Invariably, subjective questions will draw responses that are not exactly right or exactly wrong. When this occurs give partial marks.

5) Conceal your students' names while marking. This will protect them from any biases (conscious or unconscious) that you might have.

## RESEARCH IDEAS

Although we believe a final exam is important, it is not the only way to evaluate students. With some classes and some students, alternatives to final examinations might be a good choice. One of these alternatives is a directed research project. Should you choose the directed research project, here is a small sample of the kinds of research questions that would fit most texts and topics.

a. Should the Canadian government tax the products of companies that contribute to the pollution problem?

b. Research the agricultural practices of the Amish. Would their ideas about not using machinery be an important consideration for Canadians?

c. Hydroelectricity is electricity produced from water power. Although this process produces little pollution, the construction of dams to produce this water power has been controversial. Considering the environmental impacts, both good and bad, is hydroelectricity a good source of energy?

d. What function does the ozone layer perform? Can the destruction of the ozone layer be stopped or delayed?

## A FINAL WORD

We believe that neither teachers nor students should fear evaluation. In fact, both groups can benefit greatly from constant and thorough evaluation. The trick is remembering that students, like everyone else, respond to success. We believe that it is impossible to beat kids into learning through negative reinforcement and punishment. Even if it were, it would be bad in the long run. The students we know who are successful are those who eventually turn external motivation into internal motivation. We encourage you to give exams, but we encourage you even more to help get your students ready for exams.

> **"The art of being wise is the art of knowing what to overlook."**
> - *William James*

## READINGS FOR EXTENSION AND ENRICHMENT

Bangert-Drowns, Robert L. And Others (1991). Effects of Frequent Classroom Testing. *Journal of Educational Research, 85* (2), 89-99. Results indicate definite performance improvements during weekly versus biweekly testing. Students prefer weekly testing.

Boiarsky, Carolyn (1992). Using Usability Testing to Teach Reader Response (A Teaching Tip). *Technical Communication, 39* (1), 100-02. Describes an assignment in writing documentation that turns the classroom into a laboratory for usability testing, giving students a clear sense of the reader responding to their text.

Boyles, Peggy (1996). Proficiency-Oriented Testing: Reality Therapy. *Learning Languages: the Journal of the National Network for Early Language Learning, 1* (3), 14-17. Discusses the importance of appropriate proficiency-oriented testing for students studying foreign languages, explaining that grammatical accuracy is of no value if it cannot be used to carry out real-life tasks as an inherent and natural activity.

Dudek, Antoinette (1997). Testing Students with Special Needs. *Momentum, 28* (2), 30-32. Argues that rather than excuse students with special needs from testing, educators should allow them to participate, provided appropriate interventions are granted. Suggests that testing can become a valuable learning experience.

Figueroa, Richard A. Garcia, Eugene (1994). Issues in Testing Students from Culturally and Linguistically Diverse Backgrounds.

*Multicultural Education, 2* (1), 10-19. The article reviews the historical context of testing ethnic students, testing special-education students, regulatory issues surrounding the testing of ethnic pupils, and testing alternatives.

Glenn, Tom, Akin, Monta (1996). Questioning Testing: Students Monitor Own Progress in One District's Total Quality Application. *School Administrator, 53* (7), 26-28. Focusing on learning instead of testing, one school district focuses on a new system which consists of comprehensive language arts and mathematics assessments completed by students at the beginning, middle, and end of the school year.

Nickell, Pat (1993). Alternative Assessment: Implications for Social Studies. ERIC Digest. 4 p. (Report No. EDO-SO-93-1). Bloomington, IN: ERIC Clearninghouse for Social Studies/Social Science. (ERIC Document Reproduction Service No. ED 360 219). This Digest discusses three implications that changing assessment types will have for the social studies.

Potter, Les (1996). How To Improve Parent-Teacher Conferences: A Guide for Parents from the Principal. *Tips for Parents From Nassp. March 1996.* This news brief offers suggestions for developing a "parent friendly" handbook to help parents effectively prepare for teacher-parent conferences.

Struyk, L Ruth. And Others (1995). Homework, Grading, and Testing Practices Used by Teachers for Students with and without Disabilities. *Clearing House, 69* (1), 50-55. Reports results from surveys of secondary school teachers regarding what they are doing with respect to homework, grading, and testing for students with and without disabilities. Discusses implications for inclusion programs.

Tannenbaum, Jo-Ellen (1996). Practical Ideas on Alternative Assessment for ESL Students. (Report No. EDO-FL-96-07). Washington, DC: Office of Educational Research and Improvement (ERIC Document Reproduction Service No. ED 395 500). This digest provides examples of measures well suited for assessing English-as-a-Second-Language (ESL) students.

CONFORMITY is the philosophy of indifference.

**- DAGOBED D. RUNES**

You are about to take your place in an extremely complex world—the world of schools. Schools are complex institutions because of the complex people who populate them. As an integral part of this world you, the teacher, will be faced with many challenges. Your toughest year will be your first. However, there are steps you can take to help you through first-year growing pains and to insure that you stay around until you begin to reap the rewards of teaching. This section is about the complexities of schools, the challenges of teaching, surviving the first year, and celebrating the rewards of your vocation.

# CHAPTER 13

# The Complexity of Schools and Classrooms

*SCHOOLS are not only places where students come to learn; they are also places where adults work.*

**- RICHARD ARENDS**

## INTRODUCTION

If you had a nickel for everyone who asked if you became a teacher to "get the summer vacations," you'd be rich. Get used to it. It's a "crack" you'll hear repeatedly from now until your teaching career is finished. Teachers are like the old comedian Rodney Dangerfield; they get no respect.

Many people think teaching is the perfect job—9 to 3 with much vacation. You know differently. If you don't know now, you soon will. Teachers work long hours. Just how long? One study shows that teachers work 38 hours per week on in-school activities and 11 hours a week in after-school activities. We think the study is wrong. Most teachers we know work much longer outside school.

Maybe you haven't really thought about how long a teacher works. Maybe you think you already know all there is to know about schools. That's one of the problems of being a teacher. Everyone feels they know about schools because they were once students.

But viewing schools from the perspective of a student is different than viewing them from the perspective of a teacher. You, no doubt, have viewed schools from the perspective of a student but probably haven't had much chance to see them from a teacher's perspective. The purpose of this chapter is to take you on a quick trip around the desk, to the other side. What does the job of teaching look like from the other side of the teacher's desk? Here's our first answer in one word—complex.

## WHY IS TEACHING SO COMPLEX?

One reason teaching is so complex is because you work with people. Most of these people are students, but not all. An elementary teacher has about 1000 interpersonal interactions with students every day. Secondary teachers interact with as many as 150 different people per day.

What makes each of these personal interactions so difficult is that most of them are very meaningful. What a teacher does and how a teacher acts matters to the people to whom, or for whom, the teacher does or acts. A second reason why these interactions are often so difficult is that they happen quickly. Generally you have little time to think seriously about what you do. Teachers are always, it seems, "flying by the seat of their pants."

> "Everything educates, and some things educate more than others."
> - *Alice Freeman Palmer*

This makes teaching different from most other jobs. You don't always have the luxury to think about what you do before you do it. During a day, you will make hundreds of decisions to act this way or that way; but the decisions come so quickly that you will have little opportunity to observe and reflect on what is really happening. Except for those quick decisions about classroom management that all teachers must make constantly, it will be only over the long term that the decisions you make will show their true impact on the lives of your students.

While teaching, you will have little time to consider your own teaching. And, unfortunately, don't you expect help from others—even those other teachers around you who are your friends and colleagues. It probably seems silly to an outsider, and it seems a little odd to us as well, but the fact is that even though teachers all work in one place, they seldom really work together. They are surrounded by other teachers, but they rarely have time to observe these other teachers or talk with them about what they are doing.

A second reason for its complexity is that teaching is a lonely job. Teachers are not only busy; they are alone. It is not the "busy-ness" that kills the teacher. Most teachers expect and are used to hard work.

It is the loneliness. In the middle of the teaching day; in the middle of a sea of humanity; in the middle of the swirling action of children and bodies it suddenly strikes you—what you want most in the whole world is another adult to talk to. It's not that you don't like your children; it's just that they are not adults. They can always be friendly, but they can seldom be friends.

When you are finished with your teaching day, you go home. At first, a loving spouse puts up with "teacher talk." But this tolerance lasts for about a week! Failing to have another counselor, you talk your husband's ear off. Or your wife says to you: "Yeah, to death do us part, but be quiet about teaching. You're driving me nuts."

There is an informal taxonomy of "Reaction to Teacher Talk." First, for a short time, there is tolerance. Following the tolerance come physical manifestations of intolerance. These can be seen by rolling eyes, angry looks, leaving the room while you are talking, or rolling over and going to sleep. After the physical manifestations of intolerance come verbal manifestations of intolerance. You are told that "Tonight, no teaching talk." "There are important things going on in the world" or "We just want to talk about the family." Verbal manifestations of intolerance are followed by unilateral constitutional agreements. These come in the shape of rules that you have absolutely no say about. "No talking about teaching!" "No inviting other teachers over!" Soon you hit the final level of the taxonomy: isolation from all other teachers. Your spouse may say something like: "The mandatory teacher Christmas Party, but that's all." "I love you, but...just shut up about teaching." Or, in radical cases, "You will never be allowed to talk to another teacher as long as you live."

You think we're kidding? Ask a teacher! Living with a teacher is tough. Why? Because teachers are consumed by teaching. Teachers can wear you out if you let them. It's more than a job; it's a life. But it's a lonely life. And it's a complex life. But most of us choose this life because we think being a teacher is the best life we can choose. It is also a noble life. It is a life filled with dignity. We want to be teachers. And we want to do it well.

## SCHOOLS ARE COMPLEX INSTITUTIONS

Maybe we shouldn't use the word **institution**. It is foreboding, isn't it? Big. Sterile. Medical. Prison-like. But in many ways it works. **Institution** is an appropriate word especially if a teacher thinks things aren't going well. And, **institutionalized** is a feeling that comes more than occasionally.

One thing that makes schools complex is that they are institutions. An institution has a history. Each school has its own history. As well, schools have a collective history. Both of these come to play in your work as a teacher. The school itself may be small, but its history is large.

Schools have existed in North America for hundreds of years. They are part of the culture of our society; and, they have their own cultures. Everyone knows what schools are like. They are one of the most constant institutions of our society—almost a metaphor for who we think we are as a people. The values, beliefs, and expectations of schools are well known to all and have developed and grown over time.

Teachers often say that the classroom is yours, "once you close the classroom door." In many ways that's true. Still, things happen in the classroom that have walked through the classroom door, even if it is shut. The teacher may act in particular ways, but often life outside the teacher's sphere of influence affects students in powerful ways.

For example, the way schools evaluate or place students in particular classes, based on ability, makes a particular statement to a child, to parents, to administrators, to other colleagues, and to the economic community of our society. Frequently, the quiet voices of the school whisper in the ears of students so often that the statements are never forgotten by a student. How many times can you hear a voice of authority that goes unquestioned without coming to believe what that voice says? Sometimes the voices of school tell kids that they are losers; sometimes it works the other way around. Either way, these voices are powerful. What a child learns in school is not always bad, but it is not always good either.

Schools are highly visible institutions. Not only do their buildings stand erect and tall within the community, but many newspapers report what happens there. Budgets are open to public scrutiny. School Board meetings are held in an open, public community. And the principal's office is often a mini-court room where little dramas of life play themselves out before a very interested and concerned public. North America meets itself in the school. And, in North American schools, things are done in the open.

Everybody cares about schools. In North America, it is a long and honorable tradition to care about schools. One has only to study the history of schooling to become awestruck. Well before there was a need for schooling, for literacy, or for formal education, parents had the foresighted belief that education was important. They sacrificed to send their children to school even when it

> **"The good old days are now."**
> *- Milton Caniff*

would have been better in the short term to keep them home to work on the farm — when another body was more valuable than another mind, when it was hand-to-mouth tough going, and when the physical and economic quality of life was not improved one bit by learning to read and write. Still, North American parents sent their kids to school. Why? Because they had a vision of a future where education would be important to their children. It was amazing foresight.

Consider how important school is to parents before you become a teacher.

We live in a democratic society and in a democracy schools are open societal institutions. That's all there is to it. It's the honorable way to live. This openness may be, at times, troublesome for teachers; but, in general, it is positive. It has helped maintain strong public support for schools and school systems. But what is good for school as an institution is not always good for you as a teacher. This openness makes the job of teaching complex. It leaves formal schooling vulnerable to unfair attacks and the political whims of outsiders. It also keeps you, the teacher, on your toes. When you look at this little system of checks and balances from the outside, all in all it's not a bad thing. Too bad you're on the inside, on the other side of the desk now.

Schools are schools. There are no other institutions like them in society. But they are also like all other organizations in some ways. Schools strive for goals. They require membership. Principals, teachers, and students must have special qualifications if they are to go or to remain in school.

Within the institution of school, similar to other institutions, people are rewarded for success and punished for failure. There is a wide variety of workers and a broad division of labor within schools. School staffs may include nurses, janitors, curriculum coordinators, counselors, administrators, and of course students. Teachers may specialize according to grade or subject matter. Students may be separated into "streams." If you considered school as a business, you would have to say that it is a complex business.

Schools are also unlike other organizations in some ways. Unlike businesses, schools easily tolerate divisiveness and ambiguity of goals. Schools are not like department stores. The bottom line is not the cash flow or the red or black ink. Schools seem to function perfectly well—OK, nothing is perfect—even when there are many different ideas about what success means. Is it good grades? Is it self-esteem? Is it academics or vocations? The point is that there are conflicting conceptions of the purpose of schools. And, in the face of this confusion, schools still function.

You may not think that this goal confusion exists in schools. Let's give you a long-standing example that affects how teachers and students live in the classroom. Historically, one important goal conflict in the schools is whether they should emphasize academic or vocational learning. This conflict poses some important questions: "Is a classical, liberal arts education best, or should education prepare students for a world of work?" Another: "Should schools build character, or competency?" There have been battles, but up to now the war has not been won.

School is the place to be—even if you would rather be somewhere else. Schools are the institution where youngsters hang out. Society has vested in schools the role of custodian of young people. Schools are ordered by rules that force compulsory attendance. These rules are necessary, of course, because society feels that without them students would not attend. What does this mean for you as a teacher? What is the result of compulsory attendance? The answer: it is possible, even likely, to have large numbers of unmotivated students in your classrooms.

Schools are complex because they are anthropomorphic. Schools are alive; they have personalities. Schools are not all the same. Most operate under the direction of some very interesting and esoteric norms. Some schools are friendly and open. Some schools involve students as active participants. Other schools are more reserved and formal. Some schools direct students to sit down, be quiet, and write notes. Some schools encourage new ideas and experimentation. Few risks will be tolerated in others. Some encourage making mistakes because it is the way one learns. Others will tolerate no mistakes at all.

Schools may be formal institutions, but they are not so huge that they cannot be moved. Despite the formal structure of schooling, teachers continue to have a great deal of influence on schools. In our experience, the old saying mentioned earlier in this chapter is true. **Teachers can do pretty much as they please once classroom doors are closed.** In the culture of schooling, strong sanctions exist against interfering with other teachers. This may be good for teachers who have been around forever and seem to have it all together. But as a young teacher trying to learn the ropes of school, you actually hope for a little friendly interference occasionally. Sometimes you want help!

## STUDENTS ARE COMPLEX PEOPLE

Students are like snowflakes. No two are alike. This is not difficult to understand. You will learn it quickly when you meet your first class. The interesting thing to us is that schools seem to believe they can ignore this plain fact. Most schools set up classrooms as if every student were exactly alike. Students use the same textbooks, take the same notes, are treated the same way, take the same tests, listen to the same teacher who teaches in the same way, and on and on.

> "Human nature has a much greater genius for sameness than for originality."
> - *James Russell Lowell*

Sameness, even in the face of obvious lack of similarity, is the logic of schooling. Even though it is not true, it is easy to understand the logic for schools making it true—at least pretending that it is true. It is also easy to understand why teachers—the very people who know better—act as if they didn't know better. If you didn't, how could you teach within the institutions that are set up this way? Treating students as if they are the same allows teachers to teach.

But, students are all different. As a teacher, you will face an enormous variety of student differences—some obvious and some not so obvious. These differences will include culture, race, religion, socioeconomic level, home life, and intellectual ability. During your career, you will probably also teach physically-disabled, learning-disabled, latch-key children, gifted, socially aggressive, and alcohol and drug abusing students. In some of your classrooms, you will have students who can't read. In the very same classroom, you will teach children who are smarter than you. When we say this, we are not criticizing your intellect at all.

Students can and do affect the complexity of the situation. They have brains, and they do think. They can manipulate teachers, and they often do. As a teacher, you will be involved in a situation of mutual impact. You will change them, and they will change you.

Another thing that makes students different is where they come from. Students have a history before they come to school and a future after they leave school. What do your students do at home? What are their families like? We are not suggesting that you should be a social worker, trying to compensate for every student's problems. Instead, we are saying that there's more to life than school for your students. There may be a reason why one or more aren't doing homework. It might not be an acceptable reason to you, but it is a reason to consider.

You should also know that the environment of the school and the classroom directs students to act in particular ways. Something as simple as a seating pattern can have major impact on the way students behave in your classroom. Adams and Biddle have researched classroom structures and discovered what they call an "action zone." This is the area of a classroom where the activity of the class happens. It is in the middle front row seats and extends directly up the middle isle. They watched classrooms and saw that a pattern of activity could be traced. In other areas, there might be things happening, but it isn't the stuff you want to happen.

So, schools are complex because everything that happens in a classroom has an impact on teaching. Schools are also complex because everything that happens to students, both in school and out of school, has an impact on how these students live in the classroom. Even a thing as simple as a seating plan has an impact. It not only affects communication, it changes peer relations. It integrates and it segregates. It changes the way things happen.

## THE CURRICULUM IS COMPLEX

Finally, schools are complex because the curriculum is complex. As mentioned in an earlier chapter, there are at least two types of curriculum: (1) the overt, formal curriculum that you will be expected to teach and (2) the hidden curriculum that exists in the school. You will see the formal curriculum expressed in government documents and legal programs of study. Gone are the days when the philosopher-teacher held court in the agora. As a teacher, the content you will teach is usually "given from above."

> **"We don't need a teacher-proof curriculum, but a curriculum-proof teacher."**
> *- Ken Jacknicke*

There is also a hidden curriculum in schools. You will see this curriculum expressed in the local and unspoken, but very powerful, ideas about how students act within the school. But the hidden curriculum also pushes beyond the individual school. The society we live in has a logic and a system of rewards that it dishes out. Everybody knows it and almost everybody agrees with it. This is why we allow the segregation of students into different ability-levels or streams. It is this hidden curriculum that allows us to pose questions like: What makes girls successful in school? Why haven't they done as well as boys in math?

Part of the answer to these questions lies in the powerful ways the hidden curriculum of society shapes the way people think. Many of the crucial discipline problems you will face as a teacher start with the impact of this hidden curriculum on the lives of students. These students realize, maybe not consciously, that there is a logic to the society in which they live and that the school fits people to this logic. They also realize, maybe not consciously, that they do not fit this logic well. The schools are doing them no favors. As a result, they are growing up to live in a society that has a logic at which they cannot succeed. And they probably never will. How frustrating that must be.

Can you imagine what these students must be thinking? The answer is that you probably cannot. You have probably achieved success in school. Otherwise, you would not be reading this book now, preparing to become a teacher. You are one of the lucky ones for whom the society of school was constructed. Can you recall some of your classmates in elementary and secondary school who were not so lucky? How would you describe their school experience? Was it an experience you would recommend for anyone? Our advice: remember how lucky you are and all those who are not as lucky as you.

Curriculum is a plan of education in action. Students are involved in programs. These programs are seen in the classroom but they are also seen outside the regular classroom. Students may be pulled from classes for additional work. Sometimes the work is remedial; sometimes it is for gifted students.

Curriculum manages and uses time. The curriculum allocates time. Some subjects get more time than others. Such decisions may be made either by the teacher or they may be curriculum directed. You may think that increased time is a benefit for a course or program of study. But increased time does not always correlate with increased achievement. Like other aspects of life, the quality of time spent is more important than how much is spent. Engaged time is a more sensitive indicator than allocated time.

## A FINAL WORD

As a teacher you must know yourself. What are you like? What do you like? What can't you stand? Where are your soft spots? What should you guard against? These are all important questions. We think they are the most important. One of the things that makes this book different from other books you might read is that we believe that you, the teacher, are the most important cog in the wheel. Other books seem to make you believe that once you have the right technique, you can teach. We think that teaching technique is important. But it is not as important as you are.

Knowing yourself will help you realize that you will react differently towards different students. Such things as the gender, ethnicity, or ability levels of your students do make a difference. You will respond to these differences differently. Some teachers don't believe this to be true. They think that they treat all children the same—equally. It simply isn't the truth. Remember your own career as a student. How did the teachers act? If you are like most people, you will remember that teachers had "favorites." Did they mean to? Sometimes they did. Most times, we think, they did not. It happens. You will find things about some people that you like. You will also find certain things about some people that you will not like. It's human and unavoidable. What we are saying is to be aware of this and to watch yourself carefully. What impression are you giving students?

Teachers must model logical thinking and problem-solving behavior. They must show that they believe in learning and love their subject matter. They must exhibit curiosity and interest. They must show respect for others, interest in students, emotional control, and communication skills.

Do you still want to be a teacher? We hope that you do. We wrote this chapter not to scare you but to clarify the complex roles and the complex interactions that teachers much face every day. Many people cannot stand the complexity. But there is wonderful hope. There are some people who seem to thrive on the complexity; people who seem to be able to transcend the noise and to get right to the heart of the matter—teaching students and helping them grow. It is a difficult and complex job, but it is far from impossible. We hope you are the kind of person who can rise above the noise of the complex educational system, the complex school, and the complex interactions of the classroom. We hope you are learning to become a good teacher.

## READINGS FOR EXTENSION AND ENRICHMENT

Goff, Katherine E. (1998). Chaos, Collaboration, and Curriculum: A Deliberative Process. *Journal of Curriculum & Supervision, 14* (1), 29-42. Presents curriculum as a complex social process. Explores chaos theory as a metaphor for understanding curriculum and a framework for viewing the curriculum-development process.

Kreuger, Thomas (1997). Oral Communication Skills Necessary for Successful Teaching: The Students' Perspective. *Educational Research Quarterly, 21* (2), 13-26. Responses from 296 undergraduate students emphasize the importance of message and listening aspects over physical aspects.

Licklider, Barbara L. (1995). The Effects of Peer Coaching Cycles on Teacher Use of a Complex Teaching Skill and Teachers' Sense of Efficacy. *Journal of Personnel Evaluation in Education, 9* (1), 55-68. Reports on the effects of a peer-coaching in-service model on teachers' use of a complex teaching technique and the perceptions of 11 teachers and 2 principals. Results demonstrate that the peer-coaching model shows promise for increasing teacher effectiveness.

McCabe, Nancy (1995). Twelve High School 11th Grade Students Examine Their Best Teachers. *Peabody Journal of Education, 70* (2), 117-26. Reports that the best teachers care about their students as well as the subject matter.

Walker, Annie M. (1994). At-Risk Students Are People, Too. *English in Texas, 26* (1), 48-49. Argues that at-risk students have the same hopes and aspirations as other students.

# CHAPTER 14

# U sing Computer Technologies in Teaching

*SINCE we have no choice but to be swept along by [this] vast technological surge, we might as well learn to surf.*

**- MICHAEL SOULE**

## INTRODUCTION

This chapter discusses the impact of educational technologies in education and classrooms, offers suggestions about how teachers and students might use these technologies more effectively, and suggests strategies for using technology to improve teaching. We also offer a few ideas about how teachers can develop support systems to help implement technology use into their teaching and how they might change classroom and personal practices in ways that make it more possible to use technology to do their jobs better.

We are optimistic towards using technological tools in classrooms. Our own experience and the experiences of others we have known and read about tells us that computers can help teachers and students in many practical and educational ways. We begin our look at computer technology by seriously discussing the importance of technological and computer literacy and by pointing out the gulf between what is and what could be, between the available and the practised. We believe that, if computers are to be used effectively as creative tools, more than lip service must be paid to the real needs of teachers and students.

## INFORMATION AGE OPTIMISM

We are told we live in an Information Age that processes information at a dizzying speed. Sadly, most of us seem to want to match the pace of our fastest computers and to live and work at the same speed. This choice, among other choices we make, forces us to be increasingly dependent on high-quality, accurate information.

Now we have a problem. With computers, "too much" is as problematic as "too little." We can almost drown in a sea of information that hits us like waves – one ever larger than another. The information we gather, at best, is fragmented by different formats and media, qualitatively questionable, and exists in many different physical locals at once. Accessing and using this information means more than just knowing where to find it. Finding "stuff" is the easy part. The real task is to find and use the "right stuff." To use resources effectively, we must become information literate; we must know how, what, when, and even why to access and use certain information.

Librarians were perhaps the first to understand the change that came with the Information Age. The American Library Association's mission statement for the global information society defines 21st century information literacy as the ability to seek and effectively use information resources. This includes both the knowledge of how to use technologies and the forms in which information is stored. This definition implies asking good questions and accessing, locating, evaluating, and using information. These are good skills – helpful for making both academic and everyday decisions.

> "The man who does not read good books has no advantage over the man who cannot read them."
> - *Mark Twain*

Although one can argue with the "get rich through gaining information" metaphor that many technology leaders use, clearly having accurate, up-to-date information helps us become informed and intelligent. In addition, there is a huge up side to the wide availability of information in the Information Age. We are optimistic that teachers can make important democratic contributions to help close the gap between the "information rich" and the "information poor" as they help students gain the ability to access, retrieve, and use information.

We have two educational goals in mind. First, we want to help teachers understand information literacy deeply enough to help them create classroom environments where students can become more information literate. We believe that the growth of computer technology and information services can help students at all levels share resources, collaborate with others, and represent their ideas electronically. We also believe that, to help students use information resources effectively, teachers must create classroom environments rich in technological and information literacy infrastructures.

Second, we want to help reconcile our vocation with our world. As we look into homes and classrooms, we see that students' lives may be filled with computer interactions, but teachers and schools have not yet come close to considering all the ways they can help students apply these technologies to their everyday lives. As a result, there remains a wide gap between what is and what could be, and between what is learned in school and how this knowledge can be applied to everyday life, and, most importantly, how this knowledge can be used to promote critical thinking.

## WHAT DO TEACHERS NEED?

We believe that information technology is more than a tool for researching, writing, and communicating with people throughout the world. It is a way of thinking about the world – an all-encompassing idea exchange of insights that influence and shape human activity on international scales. We also believe that, as schools consider distance learning and the addition of new technologies to their curriculum, ensuring students' information literacy becomes more difficult and more important than ever. To help students, we believe teachers need to re-vision and challenge traditional classroom dynamics and relationships.

Today, there are so many different (and inexpensive) information sources that teachers and students have a difficult time choosing between the necessary and the gratuitous. School libraries are morphing into integrated high-tech centres where resource-based learning expands and draws upon resources far beyond textbooks and where information literacy can both transcend and pull together traditional academic disciplines.

At the same time as we embrace these technologies, we cling to tradition. We hold dear the values of the disciplines and the disciplined way of knowing each represents. We believe in the values of honesty, humility, integrity, and even goodness – as hard as that is to define – in our own lives and in the curriculum we create for those we educate as teachers. We believe that we should not loot those human treasures called the disciplines. Instead, technologists, librarians, and teachers should work together to teach both disciplined content and the valuable skills of navigating through the complex data bases and information resources available.

Here teachers need help. Many know how to teach traditional subject area courses, but are less comfortable teaching information literacy. Teachers already recognize their need to be lifeguards as their
students swim in an ocean of information. Many teachers have
already set their education sights on creating classroom environments
that help students become self-sustaining seekers and users of information sources and digital libraries. If this curriculum goal can come
to pass, especially in those schools where students come from disad-
vantaged or lower socio-economic backgrounds and where students
previously have had little access to sources, the democratizing possibilities of schools will continue to live.

## CURRICULUM IN THE INFORMATION AGE

Curriculum planning has changed. Today's teachers are called to
build seamless curricula designed to help use a variety of information
sources (books, journal articles, web sites maintained by strangers)
and medium (print, electronic, and networked digital libraries). To
work well, these curricula must be user-centred and focus on the
skills of locating, evaluating, interpreting, and communicating information sources rather than on technical activities.

Such comprehensive curricula should help students find and use
a variety of different digital "coffers," introduce effective search strategies, teach the tools for these searches, and help students critically
evaluate the sources and information found. Teachers should also create flexible classrooms where students can expand their learning by
doing active searches, tracking new information addresses and updat-
ing old ones, and developing a personal portfolio of favourite and
useful information sources.

At its simplest, creating curricula that help students understand
research as information seeking and information retrieval is quite easy.
Teachers already know students need practical information and literacy
skills they can use in a variety of settings. A bigger problem for teachers
is to create curricula suitable for students of different academic abilities
and with diverse needs to gain their own information literacy skills.

## TEACHING IN THE INFORMATION AGE

The Information Age has a huge potential for teaching. Never
before have students had such an easy time browsing and searching
the world's repositories of information without having to leave their
classrooms. It is not surprising that libraries without boundaries are
rapidly extending traditional geographically confined libraries. What
we have not figured out completely is how many new things we can
introduce or accept without making our classrooms so confusing that
they bewitch our students.

We believe there is a way to shake hands with change without losing one's soul. We also believe schools can not and should not quickly change their ideals of what counts as knowledge and who should decide what knowledge counts. Our great task as teachers remains to help our students learn to interpret the knowledge they collect and use.

The teachers we know seldom consider themselves moral authorities. However, all good teachers who use today's technologies are concerned with the ease with which untrained users can directly search sources and find, well, who knows what. Much of what they find lacks refinement. But even if all the information found were of high quality, how can teachers help students decrease the difficulty of utilizing information retrieval systems and get their heads around what they find?

## THE DEMAND TO KEEP UP WITH TECHNOLOGY

We often hear the dire warning that students uneducated in the modern advances of our technological society won't be prepared for the world of the 21st century. These warnings compel educators to modify curriculum to reflect the pressing needs of contemporary technology. You must keep up! To remedy this "lack of preparation" and to "keep up," school technology programs are being rapidly developed to reflect the perceived needs of our technological society.

To old teachers like us, these warnings seem recycled. In the past, the push for schools to "keep up" with technology was the genesis of an industrial trade – or industrial arts – curriculum, different for young men and women. Today, "keeping up" with technology often means teaching content derived from the world of business and modern industry. We believe

> **"I do not fear computers. I fear lack of them."**
> *- Isaac Asimov*

this is exceedingly narrow. Could it also be that the business world has an economic agenda? We hope to encourage a broad definition of technology education that encompasses holistic approaches to education; but we do not want to dump the storehouses of humanity currently protected in curriculum content.

Technology education should expand the curriculum – not eradicate it. What manner of Luddite would resist the inclusion of computers and their accompanying technologies such as Internet, e-mail, and all manners of virtual communications into school curricula? Also, as noted previously, we believe today's technological education has the potential to democratize schools. Perhaps we will no longer "need to" stream away the intellectual "have-nots" into segregated curriculum "reservations" with different expectations of academic success. Because technology education naturally brings together the intellectual and applied experiences of students, it can help establish a place where curriculum can be integrated and commonalties explored. Technology education can enhance classroom teaching by offering teachers the opportunity to integrate areas of study and bring practical and realistic student learning into the classroom.

## HOW COMPUTER TECHNOLOGIES SHAPE CLASSROOMS

Teachers who use computers must change their instructional approaches. Using computers forces teachers to focus on the structure of the information being taught, the design of the technology used to teach that information, and differences in how people learn. For example, good teachers must attend to individual abilities of students as these students interact, essentially, with a non-thinking reality. Otherwise, students may become increasingly frustrated with computers.

> **"We have become a people unable to comprehend the technology we invent."**
> - *Association of American Colleges*

Good teachers must also differentiate between the knowledge and skills that must be learned in school and the critical and creative thinking and problem-solving abilities that must be taught so that knowledge can be learned. Computer technologies do change things! They move the focus from the specific subject area knowledge as a collection of "facts" and relocate it on investigatory methods of solving problems and instructional research.

If teachers are to teach students to investigate and inquire, they must place the focus on the structure and organization of the investigation. The process, not the product, is key. Teachers would focus less on what subject area content students should know and more on how to use subject area content in relevant ways. Using technology in teaching means integrating investigatory, creative, and critical skills that use subject area content in life's situations. The interaction between students, teachers, and computer technology becomes more complex, and the relationships between academic learning and learning for everyday life and "real" work becomes more necessary.

## WHAT DO TEACHERS NEED TO KNOW?

Most teachers need to know "how-to" technology. They need to understand how to match specific systems and needs, as well as how to implement technology in ways that improve teaching. Because it is new, teachers and students need support as they implement technology. But mostly, teachers need to consider how computer technologies help them attend to their students' needs to think more critically and engage in more advanced problem-solving – especially in the face of what seems to be an increasingly more complex, post-modern society. We believe that, as computer technologies move into classrooms in an aggressive way, teachers need to hold to their fundamental ideal of the importance of progress as one of the significant products of schools and learning. Sometimes it seems so easy to get lost in the glitz and forget the basic reasons why children attend school and teachers teach. Teachers need to learn how to use technology to help them support students' academic and social success. The increased expansion of computer technologies begs thoughtful educators to re-think the future of education and debate what schools and teaching could become. As always, a teacher's focus is immediate and narrow – on the particular students within a classroom and how to encourage and guide these students toward academic success and good decision-making.

## INTEGRATING COMPUTER LITERACY INTO CLASSROOMS

Teachers have many difficult responsibilities. First, they must know where their students are academically and where they need to go. This includes understanding students' special needs. They must choose the proper activities and materials to teach their students, and they must create and administer the rules that govern student participation. Finally, they must mediate the academic expectations of parents and the community and adhere to the norms and rules that govern their actions as teachers.

Schools cannot simply add technology to classrooms and expect a quick transition. The addition of any new technology will further complicate the lives of teachers and students and presents many new questions.

Both the public and educators agree that students need to be "computer literate." But, it is not clear what it means to be computer literate. For example, is a student who can beat a computer game computer literate? How about a student who can use computer-assisted instruction? Does a student who buys and sells sport cards on eBay, or who downloads and creates an entire music library on Napster have the skills necessary to prosper in society? Does computer literacy mean students can do word processing well enough to enter the workplace or post-secondary education? As teachers, we once argued these basic educational questions often. Today we seem to have fallen into a "wait and it will take care of itself" mentality. Is it possible that we just don't know the answers to the questions computer technologies pose?

What we do know is that, in many schools, teachers and students use computers narrowly – similar to the way teachers from our childhood once used flash cards or worksheets. It appears that the computer as a tool of productivity remains sadly underdeveloped. The computer and other educational technologies, if they hold promise at all, hold promise when they are used to further subject area content, as tools to discover and synthesize information, and as ways to yield first-class presentations and representations of knowledge.

Not 20 years ago, students were learning "turtle logic," working hard learning to program computers to do simple things. Now we use computers like we use automobiles; few people know how they work "internally" but more people use them to take care of their everyday needs. Most educators believe computer skills are taught best in the context of actual work and in conjunction with the conventional, well-defined academic activities of the classroom – activities like writing, reading, and researching. What computers and computer technologies can do very well is expand and extend these activities.

## TEACHING COMPUTER TECHNOLOGY IN CONTEXT

Our reading and experience tells us that computer skills and technology should not be taught in isolation, and that separate "computer classes" do not really help students learn to apply computer skills in meaningful ways. Students sit through these classes and dutifully attend to a plethora of homogenised classroom assignments, then they go home and use computers to e-mail their friends, listen to their music, and download information about their favourite celebrity. While these activities may be well and good, students remain ignorant (not stupid) of the wider possibilities and opportunities thoughtful teachers can give them about how to use computer technology in creative and self-educational ways.

We are not alone in calling for a re-thinking of how computer technologies are taught. There have been important recent shifts in how computer technology is approached and emphasized. But in the everyday life of a classroom teacher, moving from using computers to skill-and-drill isolated facts to an integrated approach that uses computer technology to expand conventional school curricula is an important step that needs a great deal of planning and effort.

Beginning slowly in the early 1980s, educators began to move away from teaching isolated computer skills to teaching integrated information skills. Most successful were attempts to integrate information skills in activities designed around projects where curriculum was a collaboration of computer literacy skills and subject area content.

We believe that students need to learn to use computers flexibly, creatively, and purposefully. Similar to other students, students working with computers should be able to determine their own educational goals and be able to tell if a computer will help them reach these goals. Finally, they should be able to use computers to help them accomplish their goals. Individual computer skills take on a new meaning when integrated with personal problem-solving processes, and students develop true "computer literacy" as they genuinely apply computer skills as part of their everyday learning.

## HOW COMPUTERS HAVE CHANGED CLASSROOMS AND SCHOOLS

Often people equate technology with computers, but a technology is basically a tool for doing something else. Teachers have been utilizing technologies forever. For example, some common "ancient" technologies include the printed word, chalkboards, overhead projectors, telephones, audiotape recordings, slide projectors, and VCRs.

> "Our way of life has been influenced by the way technology has developed. In future, it seems to me, we ought to try to reverse this and so develop our technology that it meets the needs of the sort of life we wish to lead."
>
> *- Prince Philip*

Technological advances, especially the Internet, have opened structural restrictions that once affected classroom education. Suddenly, students have gained almost unlimited out-of-body "soaring capacities" that make old structures obsolete. Students can now access a library of knowledge of unknown quality using computers chained to their classroom desks.

Technological innovations have done more than provide a wider range of information to students and teachers. They have qualitatively altered teacher-student relations and have cultivated a networked community extending far beyond the classroom. Imagine the multiple ways a simple tool like e-mail can supplement classroom discussion.

Each innovation brings a new set of problems and issues for teachers and schools. For example, helping students stay up-to-speed with technology takes time. Imagine, as well, the incredible critical thinking skills necessary if students are to be taught to sort wisely through the enormous amounts of information on the Internet. Growing availability of technology also begs the enduring question thoughtful teachers face daily: "Is it possible to give some students too much control?"

## THE IMPACT OF THE COMPUTER ON STUDENT-TEACHER RELATIONSHIPS

How does the use of computer technology change the student-teacher relationships of the classroom? First, it calls for new power relationships between teachers and students. We can no longer assume, by virtue of experience and age, that a teacher is the most knowledgeable person in the classroom. It might well be that a student is far ahead of the teacher in areas of technological knowledge. If so, how should technologically superior students be treated? Who, after all, really knows more?

Teachers are left negotiating status, collaboratively engaging knowledge, and actively sharing power with students. Teaching, at least, demands more democratic classroom management. By this, we do not simply mean the rules of disciplined behavior in the narrowest sense of "does a student behave in class." Discipline perhaps falls back to its more classic meaning of a willed way of behavior – as in the discipline of science. And classroom management expands its narrow sense of controlling behavior to mean the developing of an ordered classroom life – as in the management of a personal stock portfolio. All in all, teachers must consider a wide array of components of individual accomplishment, knowledge, personality, and teaching style. Information technologies almost beg for qualitatively different teaching methods.

New technologies also allow teachers to create new evaluation techniques for themselves and their students. For example, teachers can videotape themselves or their students in the midst of classroom activity, using different formats for conferencing and evaluation. Such technologies offer teachers a historical log where students have opportunities to demonstrate improvement in their skills and knowledge to use learning strategies. We know that students' learning is enhanced when they can communicate using e-mail. We also know that using the Internet is a valuable aid to research. How can these two things be brought together to help students learn and teachers teach?

> "When all you own is a hammer, every problem starts to look like a nail."
>
> *- Abraham Maslow*

Those of us who engage in student-teacher e-mail relationships know exceedingly well that both the relationship and the workload is changed. Sustaining e-mail interactions with students is extremely time consuming, although it creates numerous benefits for both students and teachers. In addition, the emphasis on using technology for creating communication does carry over to the classroom, granting greater status to students, and sometimes teachers, as "technology experts" among their peers.

## WHAT COMPUTER SKILLS SHOULD STUDENTS KNOW?

To help things work effectively, teachers can help their students learn to evaluate the value of different electronic resources for data gathering - including databases, CD-ROMs, commercial and Internet online resources, electronic reference works, and electronic information resources put out by community and government. Students should learn to apply evaluation criteria that helps them judge computerized electronic resources. They should learn to evaluate the value of e-mail and online discussion groups (listservs, newsgroups) as part of a search of current literature or in relation to information-seeking tasks. And they should be able to use a computer to generate flow charts, time lines, organizational charts, project plans and calendars which help them plan and organize complex tasks.

Students should learn to use the computer resources and technologies of the school, including online catalogs and periodical indexes, full-text sources, multimedia computer stations, CD-ROMs, scanners, and digital cameras. They should then be sent out via Internet to locate and use computer resources and technologies beyond the school. Some of these include web sites housed on the different search engines; online public access library catalogues; commercial databases and online news and magazine services; and community, academic, and government resources. Students should know the roles and computer expertise of people outside the school library who might provide information or assistance.

Because they are so inexpensive, and sometimes free, students should learn to use electronic reference materials like encyclopaedias, dictionaries, biographical sources, atlases, databanks, thesauri, almanacs, and other fact books. These are available on local area networks, stand-alone workstations, commercial online vendors, or the Internet. Students should be able to use the Internet or commercial computer networks to contact experts, help and referral services. Students might also learn to conduct electronic surveys conducted through e-mail, listservs, or newsgroups.

Students should be able to use electronic information systems such as indexes, tables of content, user's manuals, graphic clues, icons, cross-references, Boolean logic, time lines, hyperlinks, and URLs - including CD-ROMs and online databases. They should also be able to use Internet search engines like Google, Yahoo, Lycos, and WebCrawler.

Students should be able to connect and operate the computer technology they need to access information and read the on-line or print materials that help them complete these tasks. They should learn to view, download, decompress, and open documents and programs from Internet sites. They should be able to cut and paste information from electronic sources into personal documents, correctly citing their work. They should learn to use word processors to take notes. They should be able to record electronic information and track the locations of the sources while being aware of proper citations, footnotes, endnotes, and bibliographies. They should learn to use spreadsheets, databases, and statistical software to process data. Finally, they should be able to analyze electronic information in the context of their work, rejecting irrelevant information.

Students should learn to classify and group information on a word processor, database, or spreadsheet. They should learn to use word processing and desktop publishing software to create printed documents, as they learn keyboard skills. They should create or use computer-generated graphics and art from electronic sources. They should be able to use electronic software to create their own spreadsheets. They should learn to generate charts, tables, and graphs using electronic spreadsheets and graphing programs. They should use file management software to create their own databases, and they should learn software such as PowerPoint or HyperStudio to create electronic presentations and to generate overheads. They should be able to create hypermedia productions, using digital video and audio. They should learn to create Web pages using hypertext mark-up language (HTML).

Students should practice using e-mail and other communications that help them share their work. They should be able to cite properly and credit electronic sources of information in footnotes, endnotes, and bibliographies. Students should learn to evaluate both the content and format of electronic presentations. They should use spell and grammar checkers to edit and revise their work. They should understand the need to act legally and ethically as they work with information technology, careful not to engage in copyright violations or plagiarism. They should use proper etiquette on e-mail, newsgroups, and the Internet.

Finally students should learn to use e-mail and online listservs and newsgroups to communicate with others about their assignments and other problems. Students should learn to use desktop conferencing, e-mail, and groupware software on local area networks to communicate with teachers and others about their own assignments, tasks, and information problems. Finally, they should thoughtfully consider new insights as they use electronic resources and tools.

## A FINAL WORD

Teachers need to understand that computer technologies reshape how knowledge is constructed and taught. No doubt, things will continue to change. In just one example, your students' perceptions of life have been fundamentally altered by media. Television has disrupted students' links with the past and has made them more focussed on product instead of on process. We know that change will continue to happen.

> **"Computers are useless. They can only give you answers."**
> *- Pablo Picasso*

We also know that, despite the extensive use of computers in education, we know little about the impact of computer instruction on our students. Educational research is simply too young to offer long-term insight into the impact computers have on the lives of teachers and students. Some day, historians will document the history of technology, and we will read about how the computer changed our lives as teachers. But, as yet, we live without the historical perspective of where technology fits into the educational process. We do not yet understand the impact of computers or the new technologies on our future, but we are certain there are many.

**READINGS FOR EXTENSION AND ENRICHMENT**

Bitter, G.B. & Pierson, M.E. (1999). *Using Technology in the Classroom* (4th ed.). Needham Heights, MA: Allyn and Bacon. A comprehensive guide to help classroom teachers, laypersons and school personnel understand the role of computers in education.

Brucklacher, B. & Gimbert, B. (1999). Role-Playing Software and WebQuests - What's Possible with Cooperative Learning and Computers. *Computers in the Schools, 15* (2), 37-48. Examines the cooperative learning that is possible in computer settings and how this can help educators better guide students to construct meaning, to build knowledge, and to become better learners.

Eisenberg, M.B. & Johnson, D. (1996). *Computer Skills for Information Problem-Solving: Learning and Teaching Technology in Context.* ERIC Digest. Syracuse, NY: ERIC Clearinghouse on Information & Technology. URL

http://ericir.syr.edu/ithome/digests/computerskills.html.
Describes the move from teaching isolated library skills to teaching integrated information skills.

El-Hindi, A. E. & Leu, Jr., D. J (1998). Beyond Classroom Boundaries: Constructivist teaching with the Internet. *Reading Teacher, 51* (8), 694-701. Examines how the Internet can be used to support the active construction of knowledge within the classroom and can be used to create authentic literacy experiences for children.

Harris, Judi. (1999). Curriculum-Based Telecollaboration: Using Activity Structures to Design Student Projects. *Learning and Leading With Technology, 26* (1), 6-15. URL
http://206.58.233.20/L&L/archive/vol26/no1/feature/index.html.
Describes 18 major "activity structures" that can be used by teachers when they design their classroom projects.

Harris, Judi. (1998). Educational Teleresearch: A Means, Not an End. *Learning & Leading with Technology, 26* (3). Discusses telecollaboration (working with others at a distance) or teleresearch (finding and using information from distantly located data sources - most commonly online). Suggests guides to help teachers design activities incorporating online research for K-12.

Hopper, K (1999). Mastering the Invisible Technologies in Education: Who Are the Real Technology Prodigies Among College Teachers? *Educational Technology, 39* (1), 50-56. Examines computer literacy, building students' confidence in technology, real-world readiness, presentation software, word processing, e-mail, spreadsheets and databases, and information access.

Jonassen, D. H. (2000). *Computers as Mindtools for Schools: Engaging Critical Thinking* (2ⁿᵈ ed.). Upper Saddle River, NJ: Prentice-Hall, Inc. Book examines mindtools to engage learners in knowledge construction.

Morrison, G.R., Lowther, D.L., DeMeulle, L. (1999). *Integrating Computer Technology into the Classroom*. Upper Saddle River, New Jersey: Merrill. Offers an alternative approach that stresses the student's use of the computer to solve real-world problems.

Wilcox, Bonita L. Bauschard, Stefan. Osterhus, John. (1998). The Information Superhighway: How Much Fun Is It? (Professional Books). *Reading Teacher, 51 (8), 706-09*. Discusses four books that help teachers learn about technology and use it in their classrooms.

# CHAPTER 15

# The Challenges of Teaching

*BEING constantly with children was like wearing a pair of shoes that were expensive and too small. She couldn't bear to throw them out, but they gave her blisters.*

**- BERYL BAINBRIDGE**

## INTRODUCTION

For some reason or another, you want to become a teacher. You have no doubt heard stories about the terrible choice you have made. Still you persist. Maybe your parents are teachers. Maybe you have had a teacher who has inspired you to greatness, either through personal greatness or personal weakness. Maybe it's as simple as knowing exactly what you want to do with your life, regardless of what anyone may tell you. Maybe you were born to be a teacher. Whatever, you have made your decision, tentatively or maybe, or solidly.

We will not be like some others. We would never try to talk anyone out of becoming a teacher. We love teaching. We can think of nothing we would rather do, and we know that we would be emptier if someone robbed us of the chance to teach. Our purpose in this chapter is to help you think for a little while about the job—not to discourage you, but rather to assist you in making the decision of your lifetime with both eyes wide open.

Here is the truth about teaching. Your life as a teacher will be up and down, repeatedly. Teaching is sometimes wonderful, sometimes joyful, and sometimes uplifting. Sometimes you will tear your hair out. Sometimes you will cry. Sometimes students, at any age, are so precious that you can't help treasuring the experiences you share with them. Sometimes, just when you think that they couldn't care less, they prove they can.

Notice the word **sometimes**. Teaching is a series of many sometimes. Let's leave you with two sets of words. Set one: wonderful, fulfilling, uplifting, relational, happy. Set two: cruel, confusing, trying, painful, stilted, and tiring. When we think about teaching, all these words immediately come to mind. We want to suggest some of the challenges of teaching. Deciding how you will meet these challenges may be some of the most important career decisions you will make. We would say good luck, but it is more than good luck. It is work.

## CHALLENGE ONE:
## TEACHER SATISFACTION

Which teachers are most satisfied with teaching? To answer the question, let's give you some idea of the teachers who are least satisfied with teaching. Researchers have found that teachers who had not majored in education were more dissatisfied with their work and pay. This finding suggests to us that there are some people who come to teaching through a side door. If they do, and they continue to compare teaching with another occupation that they are not engaged in, they may never be happy.

The most satisfied teachers are those that get into teaching through the front door. They decide that they want to be teachers, and they set their sights accordingly. Certainly, this matches what we know. We know a large group of people who, no matter what happens, want desperately to be teachers. The finding also suggests that a person would almost have to be foolish to stumble into teaching as a last resort and expect to be satisfied.

Most teachers we know go into the job of teaching with their eyes wide open. Few of them expect instant success. They know that, no matter what they do, there will always be problems in their teaching. And, they are not too disappointed when they find that there are problems. The fact is that teaching is not much different from the rest of life. Whenever you are dealing with human beings there is always an element of unpredictability. If anything, students are more human than anyone. They are especially unpredictable.

Few teachers we know expect to get rich. Without sounding too idealistic, most of the people we know who go into teaching believe it is their "mission." It's almost like a calling, and callings cannot be ignored. Problems, when they occur, drive some people out of teaching. These are the people who lack the commitment to do the task, no matter what the problems they may face. On the other hand, people who are answering a calling are more willing to face problems.

> "At eighteen our convictions are hills from which we look; at forty-five they are caves in which we hide."
>
> *- F. Scott Fitzgerald*

But for those with the vision, troubles and difficulties almost work in the opposite way. They can be positive proof that the mission is worthwhile to pursue. A Chinese saying goes: "If I told you the road would be bumpy, and it is, at least you know you are on the right road." Most teachers go into teaching knowing that the road will, indeed, be bumpy. When the bumps occur, these teachers know they are, at least, on the right road.

Other than the regular, expected problems of the job, why do teachers become discouraged? Teachers can become dissatisfied because they are not certain what their job really is. Teaching can be a series of confusing messages. Is the first order of business to treat the "whole" child? Or are we to be interested only in academic success?

Even if we choose to believe one area is more important than another, is this kind of thinking even fruitful? Your school district may have a policy that says that academic standards are important and, specifically, that your class average must be 60%. Everyone knows that this policy means that a certain percentage of students will fail. Is it acceptable that your class begins the year with the spectre of a 60% average imposed on it from an administrative source, and that some students regardless of what they do, never have a chance to succeed? Are things like student self-esteem and academic success really ever separable?

The fact is that there are many things that no one really knows for sure. It is difficult, for example, to know just how to motivate students. Some educators believe you should motivate with a stick (punishment for not succeeding), while others believe that a carrot (looking for any little successes and rewarding them) is the best way to motivate. The mental environment of teaching is one of uncertainty. When we are dealing with phenomena so diverse and complex as human bodies and spirits, there is only one thing that we can be sure of: we can't be sure!

Let us give you a little hint. We would encourage you never to trust people who are too sure. Very little in teacher education helps teachers deal with uncertainty, and very little can. This can be disconcerting, but it can also be a positive challenge. Rather than trust a series of experts, we think that teachers must grow towards their own expertise. We call this a positive challenge because we can't think of a reason not to really consider your actions and the implications of what you do. Every one of your students benefits from your serious thought and consideration. Since our own children are in schools, we see a number of good reasons for teachers to work hard and consider their work carefully.

We have said that there are many potentially confusing things about teaching. Let us give you a short list of some of the many areas that teachers are uncertain about. Here are only a few:

1) what their students know

2) what effects their teaching has had, or will have

3) what content they should be trying to teach

4) what instructional authority they have

5) how they can improve their teaching

Regardless of any confusion, when a teacher stands in front of a class, or anywhere else in that class, and assumes control of the circumstance, we know one thing. It is best to have certain fundamental principles of teaching already worked out in your mind. These fundamental principles won't always make you certain about the situations that you come across. You will be flying by the seat of your pants much of the time. But having thought about what's important, what the job of teaching really is, what rights and responsibilities students and the school have, how you should treat others, and how you want to be treated will do one important thing. It will keep you centered on the task.

As we mentioned before, the proverb suggests that knowing the road would be bumpy helps you know you are on the right road. The best that teacher education can do for you (and this includes self-awareness) is to tell you that the road will probably be bumpy and to help you put some good shock absorbers on your car. We can't change the road, but we might be able to make the car you are traveling in more sturdy and roadworthy.

## CHALLENGE TWO:
## BECOMING SELF-AWARE

One bump in the road is self-awareness. Most teachers don't seem to know what's going on in classrooms, even their own. Teaching is like any other profession. Any busy professional has the double problem of doing a job and watching herself or himself do that job. Self-awareness is especially difficult in teaching because there is so much happening in the classroom. In teaching, the pressures of day-to-day work and the series of externally and internally imposed deadlines make self-monitoring a particular problem. If you have a teacher friend you like and trust, ask that person to watch your class and comment on what you are doing. Then, don't be surprised if what you think you are doing is not what you seem to be doing when that person watches you work.

**"I see and approve better things but follow worse."**
- *Ovid*

Research points to a gap between intentions and executions. Don't easily dismiss asking someone to watch you teach. As mentioned earlier, one of the best things you can do to grow as a teacher is to find a critical friend—one who will tell you what's really happening and someone who you are absolutely sure is your friend.

Finding and choosing a critical friend may not be easy. Critics who only stress the negative are easy to find, but you won't want them around. They will help you feel rotten, but will not help you grow. People who, generally out of fear that they will hurt you, will say that everything you do is great are also too easy to find. They may make you feel good until you realize that they are so afraid of telling you the truth that you can't trust anything they say. You don't want them either.

The kind of person who can really help is the true friend: the person you respect; the person who will tell you what is really what; and the person who really likes you. Such people are indispensable. Ask them for help. Really listen to them as they tell you what they see. And, trust their advice. It may not motivate you to change, because you may have another agenda. But don't easily dismiss the people you trust. If you really want to change, you are foolish not to listen to them.

All this means that you have to change your inside as well. If you are so self-absorbed that you can't accept criticism, even from a critical friend, then don't ask for help. If you won't trust the judgment of others whom you know care about you, then don't waste their time and energy. Try to go it alone, and good luck. You will need it.

### CHALLENGE THREE: DISCIPLINE

Whenever young teachers and teacher candidates are surveyed, one problem surfaces almost without exception. This problem is discipline. Our own research suggests that our university students have two big concerns. These can be expressed in the following questions: (1) Can I keep control of the classroom situation? and (2) Do I know my subject area well enough? Other surveys list the concerns of teachers in this order: (1) discipline, (2) student relations, (3) classroom supplies, (4) faculty relations, and (5) lesson planning.

Clearly, discipline is the worry of most teachers' lives. One thing is clear to us. Since most students you will teach are kids, it probably would be wise to expect them to act like kids. Expecting those who are not yet adults to act as adults would be foolish. We suspect that even if you could make them act as adults, it would be like a Midas Touch. In the end, you really wouldn't like it. There are so many wonderful things about teaching that are linked, without question, to the fact that the students you teach are children. In our experience, one of the best discipline techniques is to realize just whom you are dealing with and to start to appreciate the distinct advantages of your children.

> **"Shall we make a new rule of life from tonight: always be a little kinder than necessary."**
> *- James M. Barrie*

But this is not to say that part of your job as a teacher is not to encourage kids to grow into adults. In fact, the best discipline techniques we know revolve around two simple principles: (1) Students should be treated as young adults who are responsible for their actions. (2) Discipline is best handled from a preventive point of view. If you really think about these two points, they encourage some reasonable responses. First, they suggest that teachers can "reach out" and make students aware of the rules. Second, they encourage teachers to "organize for discipline" and to expect discipline to help. Teachers can, by manipulating the environment and not the students, create the kind of controlled atmosphere in their class that will actually improve the chances of learning taking place.

There is a difference between teaching discipline and disciplining. It is legitimate to expect students to mature, and a big part of maturity is self-discipline. Any discipline technique that is not connected to a growth in student self-discipline is only a temporary measure. It will not be fruitful in the long run. Many new teachers do not really understand classroom discipline. They think that what they want is for their students to be quiet. But discipline is more about teaching than it is about a lack of noise.

There are fundamental differences in how teachers discipline. Some watch for instances where students are straying from the rules of the classroom, and build a system of punishments. In some cases, a teacher may even hope that a student strays because "you can always use a good example." Some teachers work from a different set of principles. They build a system of rewards for hard work. They then look for opportunities to reward students for doing well.

The difference in these guiding principles for discipline is the difference in how people are perceived. One set of principles sees students as problems to be solved. The other sees students as growing, developing young people—immature and certainly with much to learn, including self-discipline—but not as problems to be solved. These teachers see the growth of students toward maturity as a natural state of events, one that can be encouraged and praised by a teacher, but not one that is a problem in itself.

We hope it is obvious that we believe strongly in the second set of guiding principles. Let us set out our principle clearly: for effective discipline to occur, students must perceive the teacher as someone who cares about them and wants to help, rather than the evil eye who is watching every move, just waiting to punish them. Consider the difference between these two statements:

**The Evil Eye:**
*Watching Students,*
*Waiting to Punish*
**The Caring Eye:**
*Watching Students,*
*Waiting to Reward*

We see our statement about discipline as (1) a practical statement about what works, (2) an ethical statement about the way that humans should build relationships, and (3) a political statement that reflects the only legitimate way that a teacher and a school system in a democratic country can teach. If we are indeed a country that reflects the principles of democracy and equality of opportunity, how can we teach otherwise?

In summary, what do teachers need to do to promote good discipline in their classrooms? Here's our short list, based on our own beliefs, our own experiences, and our own reading of the research:

1) Become educated people.
2) Understand and accept their role as stewards of schools in a democracy.
3) Approach their teaching reflectively and thoughtfully.
4) Possess the skills and attitudes necessary to work toward school and human renewal (that is, actively do things that promote human growth and development).

This seems like a simple list, doesn't it? Why, then, is discipline such a difficult concept to teach? The answer, in short, is this. Most people believe that maintaining order and stability is more important than educating students and encouraging social and intellectual growth. We encourage you to think of your job as a teacher as the encouraging of social and intellectual growth. If you can do this, an ordered and stable classroom will be a secondary result.

## CHALLENGE FOUR: STRUGGLING TO COMPENSATE FOR A TROUBLED SOCIETY

This challenge is one that most books do not deal with, because it does not seem to be a central task of teaching. But any teacher who works with students and who cares about students knows that there are real problems—problems that are usually said to fall outside the classroom—that play a big part in what actually happens in the classroom. Young people live in a difficult time and in a difficult society.

Things are not stable for them, and the instability causes problems. There are problems that teachers face every day. Can and should teachers do something about those problems?

The fact is that teachers have little choice except to accept the task. Statements that "teachers are not social workers" are short-sighted. We wish it weren't true. We wish that all a teacher had to do was to teach. But, the plain truth is that to go blithely about teaching without addressing in some way real problems that young people face is blindness. It just won't help students.

What is the social environment in which students live? An American research study that addressed the potential influence of teachers offers some statistics that give an insight into the adolescent experience. The study [Csikszentmihalyi, M. & McCormack, J. (1986). The influence of teachers. *Phi Delta Kappan,* 67(6), 415-419.] reported that typical American adolescents spend approximately

> 5 minutes per day alone with their fathers
> 40 minutes per day alone with their mothers
> 1 hour per day alone with both parents
> 15 minutes per day with other adults

The study also suggests what happens during this time. Almost all of this time is spent unwinding from school or work and in maintenance activities such as eating, cleaning, and shopping. The study suggests that very little important information is passed on during these routine interactions.

On the other hand, typical American adolescents spend

> 4 hours per day with their friends
> 4 to 5 hours per day alone
> 2 hours per day with the television set
> 3 hours per day with their teachers

The point of the research is this: the single most important opportunity for adolescents to learn from adults happens each day with teachers. Even if we teachers wanted to, it would be almost impossible to ignore the need to deal with problems that young people face. Young people seem to almost invite teachers to help them. When asked who or what influenced them to become the kinds of people they are, students gave the following answers:

> 58% mentioned one or more teachers
> 90% mentioned their parents
> 88% mentioned peers

More than half the young people surveyed suggested the importance of teachers to their growth and development. This research is not an aberration. Other studies echo the potential impact of teachers. Yet there is an irony in these findings. Of all places students like to "hang out," school is the place they like least to be. When they are in school, the classroom is the place they most wish to avoid. Students prefer almost any place else in the school, the cafeteria, the hallways, the library, even the washrooms.

Here's another interesting irony. Although 58% of the students suggested that teachers had most influenced them to become the people they were, students also reported that only 9% of all the teachers they had encountered during their school careers had made any difference in their lives. More than 9 teachers out of 10 (91%) were not memorable.

What makes a teacher influential? The students had little difficulty in answering the question. Students described influential teachers in terms of their abilities to generate enthusiasm for learning, that they were "easy to talk to," and that they were ready to listen when students had difficulty learning. When we think about these criteria for a minute, two thoughts come to mind. These three criteria for influence are not very hard to accomplish and ought to be a natural part of any effective teacher's job. The sad question remains: Why are teachers not accomplishing these things?

Here's a final, practical point: when teaching is effective, students not only enjoy the class but also learn to enjoy the subject matter. We call this a practical point because we believe that when teachers become influential, discipline is less and less of a problem for them. Ask yourselves the following questions: Did influential teachers first concern themselves with discipline, and second with becoming influential? or Did they want to become influential first and let discipline take care of itself?

> **"The worst sin toward our fellow creatures is not to hate them, but to be indifferent to them."**
> *- George Bernard Shaw*

Probably neither question is a good one. We suspect that effective teachers made both academic instruction and intellectual and social growth priorities of their work. They worked to build positive relationships with their students. And they simply worked through classroom life with a set of guiding principles in mind.

The building of positive and personal teacher characteristics is not new. In 1901, the city of Detroit listed a number of important points for their teachers to consider before beginning a job. At first they may seem a bit silly, but consider how many of these points are important today.

## POINTS FOR TEACHERS

1. Does your manner attract or repel pupils and parents?

2. Is your voice pleasing, or harsh and grating?

3. Are you pedantic and pretentious, or frank and dignified?

4. Are you fidgety and nervous, or quiet and equable?

5. Is your eye restless and foxy, or calm and penetrating?

6. Is your face deceitful, or pleasant and honest?

7. Is your walk hesitating and unsteady, or direct and firm?

8. Is your judgment wavering and fitful, or judicial and impartial?

9. Is your judgment narrow and selfish, or broad and liberal?

10. Is your scholarship weak and restricted, or comprehensive and accurate?

11. Is your health tottering, or is it vigorous and strong?

12. Is your moral nature weak and vacillating, or is it noble and elevated?

13. Have you stagnated, or are you still elastic and buoyant?

14. Is your attitude toward your school board one of helpful cooperation?

15. Do you recognize that they are the real authority in school matters?

16. Do you first find whether they sympathize with new plans before applying them to the school?

17. Do you follow out any suggestions they may make?

[List of Qualified Teachers and School Officers for Wayne County Michigan, 1900-1901 (Detroit: E.W. Yost, Commissioner of schools), p. 37. As quoted in Phi Delta Kappan, 67(6), 427.]

## CHALLENGE FIVE: BURNOUT

We have all heard about "burnout." Burnout is a wonderfully expressive word, even though it is probably used too often and too loosely about teachers. One of the real problems with the word is that it not only describes the tension and stress of the teaching profession, but it sets a kind of conceptual standard for stressed teachers to live up to. Like the ever-present term dyslexia, burnout can mean many things, including the normal day-to-day stresses that all jobs include.

Teacher burnout has been a topic of study for educational researchers for many years. We have known people who have burned out, and we have read some of the research about burnout. We know some things about burnout that might help you as a beginning teacher.

For one thing, we know that there are a number of important characteristics that are related to school stress and burnout. Two of the biggest difficulties teachers face are (1) role ambiguity (what are you supposed to do?) and (2) locus of control (do you have the power to do what you think is best?). Neither of these two problems is to limited teaching, but each is probably more pronounced there. But for young teachers, there's good news. Research studies suggest that young teachers are better able to handle these problems than older teachers. We hope that, by the time burnout becomes a potential problem, the rest of "your act" is sufficiently together to ward off its threat.

Research suggests that the number of years of teaching experience helps to explain the intensity of burnout and emotional exhaustion. Teachers who have taught a long time face the greatest difficulties. So, the bottom line is this. If you're worried about burnout happening in your first few years of teaching, you probably shouldn't. Your natural, youthful energy will probably get you through, at least for a while. Then, hopefully, the things you've learned about the subject you teach and the people you are teaching will make your teaching experience one that brings you great joy.

In our first draft of this chapter, we suggested that what you will have learned should get you through; but we changed our minds. Getting through is not enough. Teaching doesn't need survivors; it needs succeeders. If you are a new teacher, we want you to forget all about burnout. If you're waiting for burnout to happen to you, you probably have a while to wait.

Research also tells us that burnout is not a general thing. It does not mean the same thing to both men teachers and women teachers. Burnout differs because men and women teachers experience different teaching problems. Men experience more depersonalization. Women experience more depression, headaches, and role conflict. When studies are done about what causes burnout, there is a great variation about the reasons. Women tend to burnout for the following reasons: role conflict, marital pressures, work sources of stress, and lack of social support. For men, the principal contributors to burnout are the stresses caused by doubts about competence and problems with students.

But not all teachers face burnout. For some lucky teachers the word doesn't even spring to mind. What's the difference between teachers who burnout and those who don't? The difference is in the levels of stress that teachers face.

If you want to avoid burnout, the answer is to get rid of your sources of stress. Sounds like life, doesn't it? Researchers would say it this way: stress is negatively correlated with efficacy and internal locus of control. This is research language, but what it means in plain English is that if teachers feel they have control of what's going on, they are unlikely to experience stress. And if they are unlikely to experience stress, they are unlikely to experience burnout.

To us, the research findings seem to beg the following question: "How can teachers learn to have control over their situations?" This is not a trivial question. But the research also gives us some hints about the possible answers. Teachers who report low stress levels are those with few discipline problems, few intra-personal problems (both in and out of teaching), and good relationships with superiors, colleagues, and students' parents.

> "The greatest mistake you can make in life is to be continually fearing that you will make one."
> - *Elbert Hubbard*

What are some of the stresses of the job? You might hear a teacher say: "Teaching would be great if it weren't for the students." But research doesn't necessarily agree. It's probably more realistic to say: "Teaching would be great if it weren't for the administrators." Teachers who report that they have supportive administrators or supervisors and that they receive positive comments about their teaching skills and abilities from others were found to be less vulnerable to burnout.

In short, the same classroom problems probably exist for all teachers. It's what's outside teaching (your support group) and what's inside you (the way you perceive reality) that makes the biggest difference in whether you are able to face your problems.

How can you deal with the problems that are naturally a part of teaching? Here's what our reading of the research suggests, and we are only half kidding:

1) Develop a relationship with another teacher with whom you can talk about teaching ideas, stresses, and problems.

2) Build a mutual praise society, where the members work to renew your spirit and others' spirits by saying good things about what you do.

3) Make sure you teach in a school where the administration is supportive and caring.

4) Make sure you lay out in your own mind and with your administrator just what your job as a teacher is.

5) Make sure you are in a situation that you can control and where your actions are not constantly being reversed by others.

6) Stay young.

7) Make sure to develop good relationships with both students and their parents.

In short, the trick to surviving burnout is to take care of your inside: know why you are doing what you are doing and on what principles you are working. And take care of your outside: build the environment in which you are working by establishing good, well-defined relationships with others.

## A FINAL WORD

When you accept a teaching job, you accept the challenges that go with it. This chapter has dealt with five challenges that face teachers. They are teacher satisfaction, discipline, self-awareness, dealing with the problems of a troubled society and burnout. Certainly, there are other problems that we haven't even touched.

So, what will you do? Will the challenges scare you off, or send you in the direction of an easier job? If you have read this chapter and think that you don't have the stuff to face the challenge, we encourage you to rethink your decision to teach. You will do no one a favor, especially yourself, by continuing to seek a job where you are pretty sure you will never be happy. If you can't shake the feeling that teaching is not for you, then teaching is probably not for you. Recognize it and go on.

But if you have considered the challenges and still feel that being a teacher is what you want to do, congratulations. We applaud your decision. Still, your job is not over. And it will probably never really be over. If you have considered your choice and have chosen wisely, you are only beginning your journey. We hope this book will help and encourage you.

## READINGS FOR EXTENSION AND ENRICHMENT

Byrne, John J. (1998). Teacher as Hunger Artist: Burnout: Its Causes, Effects, and Remedies. *Contemporary Education, 69 (2), 86-91.* Examines correlations between the literature about teacher burnout and data gathered from surveys conducted at a New York high school and college.

Dinham, Steve. Scott, Catherine (1997). *Modelling Teacher Satisfaction: Findings from 892 Teaching Staff at 71 Schools.*

Paper presented at the Annual Meeting of the American Educational Research Association, Chicago, IL. Reports that teachers are satisfied by matters intrinsic to the role of teaching, such as student achievement, positive relationships with the students, self-growth, and mastery of professional skills.

Hill, Lynn T. (1995). Helping Teachers Love Their Work. *Child Care Information Exchange. 104*, 30-34. Examines three reasons teachers leave their profession and approaches for helping them to love their work. Suggests that when teachers feel challenged, in control of their lives, and have a sense of belonging, their needs have been met.

Levin, Benjamin (1994). Educational Reform and the Treatment of Students in Schools. *Journal of Educational Thought, 28* (1), 88-101. Reviews educational reform literature advocating changes in the organization of teachers' work to foster teacher satisfaction and effectiveness by treating them as reasonable, capable, and autonomous persons.

Mayer, G Roy (1999). Constructive Discipline for School Personnel. *Education & Treatment of Children, 22* (1), 36-54. Compares Constructive Discipline with traditional discipline approaches and stresses the need to clarify discipline policy, provide considerable staff support, and make allowances for individual student differences in the discipline policy.

Pool, Carolyn R. (1997). Up with Emotional Health. *Educational Leadership, 54* (8), 12-14. Reports that emotional well-being predicts success in academic achievement, employment, marriage, and physical health; and that schools must incorporate the five dimensions of emotional intelligence (self-awareness, ability to handle emotions, motivation, empathy, and social skills).

Schamer, Linda A., Jackson, Michael J B. (1996). Coping with Stress: Common Sense about Teacher Burnout. *Education Canada, 36* (2), 28-31,49. Suggests strategies to manage stress and prevent teacher burnout.

Singh, Kusum, Shifflette, Linda M. (1996). Teachers' Perspectives on Professional Development. *Journal of Personnel Evaluation in Education, 10* (2), 145-60. Reports that peer collaboration and self-awareness were most often cited by teachers as reasons for improvements in competence.

Trent, Lynette M Y. (1997). Enhancement of the School Climate by Reducing Teacher Burnout: Using an Invitational Approach. *Journal of Invitational Theory & Practice, 4* (2), 103-14. Addresses the causes of burnout and implements strategies to assist in the reduction and ultimate prevention of burnout using invitational theory as a foundation to create a better school climate.

# CHAPTER 16

# Teaching Your First Year

*IF there is anything we wish to change in a child, we should first examine it and see whether it is not something that could better be changed in ourselves.*

**- CARL GUSTAV JUNG**

## INTRODUCTION

Maybe the scariest year of your teaching career is year number one. Most teachers we know go into their first year armed with two powerful emotions: anticipation and fear. Generally, their fears—at least part of them—are rewarded. If you are like most teachers, your first year of teaching will indeed be the most difficult.

So, how do you survive your first year? Maybe the best answer is that you simply survive it. First years are not always bad, but they usually are tough. We both were first-year teachers and we think we can offer four good pieces of advice for your first year: (1) try not to make the same mistakes twice, (2) don't let your mistakes eat you up, (3) learn as much as you can, even if you can't do much about it now, and (4) unless you absolutely know after your first year that teaching is not for you, no matter how bad you think your first year was, give yourself a second chance. Re-evaluate what you are doing, make a solid plan of action based on what you have learned, and give teaching your best second shot. Then, if it isn't for you, you'll know.

First years and mistakes go together. Falling down is not the real problem. The real problem is falling down and not being able to get back up. How you see your first year experiences is probably more important than what your first year experiences were. The first year may be the most important year of your whole teaching career. Decisions that you make in this year have the potential to influence significantly your entire teaching career. So, don't make rash decisions.

We are not trying to scare you away from teaching. Nor are we trying to dash your hopes. But we must be honest. The fact is that some of you will have a great first year, although we doubt you will go through a first year without significant problems of some sort. The fact is also that many of you will have troubles your first year. Even though you may turn out to be a great teacher, you may still have troubles your first year. Why are we so sure? Because we are good teachers, and we had troubles our first years. So did our friends.

> **"Schools are now asked to do what people used to ask God to do."**
> *- Jerome Cramet*

Many people turn up their noses at idealism. They're wrong. We are idealistic. We want you to be, and we want you to stay idealistic. We believe you should start your first year with high hopes. Can you imagine how difficult it would be to survive without high hopes? Don't think you are a sap if you are idealistic and have high hopes. It is perfectly normal and right. In time, you will have experiences that shape you. These experiences will tell you which ideals to abandon, which ideals to modify, and which ideals you should steer your career by.

## WHY DO FIRST-YEAR TEACHERS HAVE PROBLEMS?

On the face of it, the answer is simple. They don't know what is going to happen. They don't have enough experience to react successfully to surprises. And they are looking at the classroom with a completely different perspective than they have before.

Most teachers, when they look back at their university career, say that their student teaching experiences were the most influential experiences they had. It is in student teaching that they begin to gain the perspective of a teacher and lose the perspective of a student.

We mentioned before that one of the problems of teaching is that the school is familiar turf. Everyone seems to know what is happening there. Young teachers, also, have a long history in school. This history can be more of a problem than a help. It is not always the strangeness of the classroom that causes problems for the young teacher. The beginning teacher's familiarity with the classroom sometimes leads to most of his or her problems. There is a feeling that says: "I have been here before. I know what I am getting into. I am no stranger to schools." But school as a teacher is not at all like school as a student. Real problems become common when the roles of student and teacher are reversed. You knew school as a student, not as a teacher.

So how will you learn about school. There are two choices. First, you can learn by yourself. You can read and consider. Or you can spend years in the classroom. Someday, many of you will suddenly realize that you have chosen a second way. This second way of learning is to learn from others. You can talk with other teachers.

In many jobs socialization and induction are the responsibilities of experienced peers, but usually not in teaching. Beginning teachers are usually left alone to struggle and survive (or fail) by themselves. Too bad. Why is it this way? Probably the answer has a lot to do with the way schools are organized. When you are a teacher, you are one person amongst many. You are in the classroom alone. That's where you will learn. It can, indeed, be tough.

## CONCERNS AND PROBLEMS OF FIRST-YEAR TEACHING

If you are like most young teachers, you will have some difficulties. You will no doubt differ from other first-year teachers in interests, personality, and talents, but you will probably have very similar problems. The difficulties teachers face are often the same from teacher to teacher.

Here's a list of the concerns and problems most often mentioned by beginning teachers:

1) classroom management and discipline
2) inability to find materials needed
3) evaluating student work
4) interacting with parents
5) feeling of isolation

Are you surprised? You may want to think about this list. We

> "The inexperienced teacher, fearing his own ignorance, is afraid to admit it. Perhaps that courage only comes when one knows to what extent ignorance is almost universal."
> *- Ezra Pound*

have already mentioned in this book some of the ways that you might best deal with management and discipline. We have also suggested how you might best interact with the people you will meet during the year. But, ultimately, you have to respond and deal with your problems by yourself.

One way to start solving your problems is to recognize that these problems will probably exist. We suggest that you begin by accepting that you will probably have problems in the five areas that are listed here. Second, we suggest that you begin to build a plan that will help you systematically solve these problems before they exist.

For example, if you know that feelings of isolation will probably be a problem, you might work toward establishing a partnership with another teacher to help solve this problem. It would be simple enough to find another young teacher and agree to meet once a week to talk seriously and honestly about the problems you are facing. First, you might reach some mutual solutions. Still, even if you don't, all is not lost. You still can become involved in an informal therapy. Really, you can't lose.

The same plan would work for most of the five things on this list. The point is that rather than hanging your head and sulking about your problems you can work successfully to solve them. There is much you have to learn on the job; but there is also much you can consider and work to solve before stepping into your first year of teaching. We promise; the effort and hard work are worth it. Teaching can't be made perfect, but it can be made easier.

## THE SURPRISES OF TEACHING

Not only are there similarities in the problems that first-year teachers face, there are similarities in what surprises first-year teachers. Here's a short list of the things that surprise beginning teachers:

1) how difficult it is to reach students (particularly in secondary schools)
2) how difficult it is to motivate students
3) the amount of paperwork
4) the amount of administrative work
5) the emotional and physical drain of teaching
6) the unprovoked hostility of students
7) the students' disdain for the subject you cherish
8) how difficult it is to manage and discipline

Again, what can you do? The answer is that, now that we have given you the list, you can prepare for these surprises before they happen. This preparation is no panacea, but it can help. Thinking about what is likely to happen and preparing for the contingency that it probably will happen is one way to either lessen the impact of the problems or, in some rare cases, help to eliminate the problems altogether. One rule of thumb is that you should not take responsibility for things (such as unprovoked hostility) over which you have no control.

## WHAT ARE THE MAJOR HURDLES
## FOR FIRST-YEAR TEACHERS?

If you are going to be a successful teacher, there are many problems that you will have to overcome. We know that you can and probably will overcome these problems, but we hope that our listing them will help you overcome them more quickly than if we would have left you on your own.

What will your hurdles be? Probably the biggest is that you will be forced to wear many different hats. Teachers have many roles they must play. They are required to be counselors, police officers, custodians, lobbyists, psychologists, comforters, bookkeepers, legal interpreters, and often parents.

You may be ready for everything about teaching, but we doubt that you will be ready for the paper work. Here are only a few of the things that you will have to keep track of during a year: test scores, homework, assignments (both written and reading), late students, attendance, unit progress, locker assignments, in-service reports, responses to requests from principals, which students belong to which parents, and your own outside life—if you have any.

From a teaching point of view, the biggest problem that first-year teachers have is that they are first-year teachers. They have neither the experience nor completed lesson plans. You may have six different course preparations in a term. Of course, that wouldn't be bad if you had all of them prepared beforehand. Then you would only have to "tweak" them, depending on your class. But, remember, this is your first year and you've never taught any of these units before. So you spend the first year worrying about the constant problems of management and worrying constantly about being prepared.

Such is the life of a first-year teacher. You will often find yourself starting from scratch. You will develop lessons and units in terms of concepts, sequencing, examples, assignments, and homework. And you will do it on top of everything else that you must be concerned about. Do you see why we have encouraged you so much to find another teacher or group of teachers to work with?

Your first year of teaching may seem to last an eternity; but, fortunately, the first year of teaching only lasts one year. Only too soon it will seem to have flown by. And the physical and mental fatigue that you experience will also go. Well, most of it.

You will learn how to pace yourself on the job. You will learn some short-cuts. Still, if you are like most, you will never grow out of the pattern of work you develop in your first year. You stay up late, marking and planning. Then you put in a full day of class and extracurricular activities. Teaching is a difficult job at the best of times. It is easy to become worn down.

First year or not, classroom discipline will always rank high on your list of worries. Certainly, as a new teacher, it will be one of your biggest concerns. Depending on your level, your style, and your classes, discipline and management will be a big concern or a little concern. But it will always be a concern. If you are going into teaching and you believe that you will never have to discipline a student, we have only one question: do you understand the concept "fat chance"? Discipline and management will always be a concern in teaching. It goes with the territory.

Another problem will be the little voice that haunts your mind. This voice asks haunting questions such as: how do you know that the students have learned anything? It's a good question. How do you insure that learning takes place? If you do not know it already, you will soon learn that there is a big difference between presenting a lesson and knowing for sure that the students have learned. Is it possible to teach, but without really teaching? Our advice: Before you get there, ask and answer the following question. "How can I know as a teacher that my students are learning?"

A third problem will be the new relationships you must establish. You will have to work with a variety of different people. These include administrators, other teachers, students, and parents. We encourage you to consider these relationships carefully. They are important because they have the potential to provide sources of anxiety or sources of support. Look around. You will need sources of support.

What if you find after a few months that you simply do not like, or cannot work in, the area assigned. You are still convinced that you should be a teacher, but just not at the school, in the area, subject matter, or at the grade level where you are currently teaching. Probably, you will have to stay where you are for the rest of the year. It would be difficult and probably unwise to change right now. Still, it's probably not the end of the world and in one sure sense you should be pleased. You have discovered something about yourself, and it's not too late to change. New teachers are often misassigned. They are put in a subject for which they are not prepared, at a grade level that is inappropriate for their strengths, or at a school where they know they will not last. Our advice: stick it out, don't cheat or rest, do the best you can, and apply for a transfer. Many good teachers make changes early in their careers.

> **"To grow is to change, and to become perfect is to change many times."**
> *- Cardinal Newman*

One common problem that is easy to fix, although many teachers don't see how, is teacher isolation. New teachers who are immersed in their work are often overcome with a sense of being alone. When the bell goes and the door is closed, it can seem as if you are imprisoned.

It's true; there are few opportunities to interact with other adults throughout the day. Our advice: Don't get caught in this problem. Know that it is going to happen and do something about it beforehand. Find a colleague with whom you can talk and talk. It will do you both good.

Finally, we encourage you not to worry about what you can't do anything about. Often new teachers feel a lack of control over the situation in which they are placed. They wonder: Which students will be in my classes? Which grade level will I teach? What subjects will I teach? It might be that the best solution is no solution at all. If there are things that are out of your control, why worry about them? It's fruitless. If there's a problem that is not of your own doing, cope but don't lose sleep. Worry about and work only on things that you can control. If you lost sleep over every problem that you had no say over, you'd be dead young.

## STARTING THE YEAR RIGHT

We'd like to give you some advice about starting the school year off right. Here are some of the things that we know. A good first impression is a good first impression. During their first meeting with you, your students size you up. They make a guess about whether you are interesting or boring, about whether you are tough or loose about discipline and management, about whether you have a pleasant personality or are cranky.

The interesting thing about this first impression is that it soon turns into a lasting impression unless drastic things happen to change it. This can be either good or bad. If you make a good first impression, fortunately it tends to last. If you make a bad first impression, unfortunately it is difficult to change. When relationships are fixed in the students' minds, they seem to stay that way.

So, then, how do you get off to a good start in the classroom? Here is some important encouragement from research coupled with the advice of good teachers. First, have as much contact with your students during opening days as you can. Don't hide. Instead, remain visible. Second, be ready to start immediately. Remember, we suggested that students like to work. Third, extend a warm welcome. Get acquainted

> "We should be careful to get out of an experience only that wisdom that is in it—and stop there; lest we be like the cat that sits down on a hot stove-lid. She will never sit down on a hot stove-lid again—and this is well; but also she will never sit down on a cold one anymore."
>
> *- Mark Twain*

with your students and help students get acquainted with each other. Fourth, make sure rules and procedures are well explained. It may seem elementary, but take the time to state exactly what you want. Our earlier suggestion still holds: most students want to do what you want them to do. They are most comfortable and less likely to push things if they know exactly where the boundaries are. Fifth, keep your list of rules short. Explain the logic behind them and why they are important. Sixth, make the first lessons enjoyable. Make them uncomplicated, but solid. These lessons should focus on the whole class working productively. Seventh, be sensitive to student needs. These needs include their attention span, level of difficulty, and the immediate environment. Eighth, exhibit good listening skills. Encourage the students to talk, and then listen to what they have to say.

## GETTING A GOOD START IN THE COMMUNITY

Although it's not as important as getting off to a good start with your students, settling your life outside school can make your life in school easier. We encourage you to consider getting off to good start in the community in which you will live. First, we encourage you to visit the school on a number of occasions before opening day. Get a lay of the land. Make driving around a habit. Take care of all the living arrangements, even if it costs you a little extra money, two weeks before you are going to start teaching.

One way to get to know the community is to conduct a driving or walking tour. You might even find a friend in the school administration to take one morning to drive you around to different spots. If you are moving to a new town, relocate in the community well before school begins to get your household set up. The point is simple. You don't need much extra grief during the first few weeks of your first year of teaching. Anything you can do to make your life easier is worth it. Think ahead.

## SURVIVING AND FLOURISHING IN THE FIRST YEAR

OK, we've told you that your first year may not be good. And it probably won't be easy. But you can and probably will survive. First, try to keep things in perspective. Be honest. Do not accept blame for things beyond your control. Some problems arise from the way schools are structured, and you can't do anything about them. But always consider the questions honestly: "Am I any part of my problems? If I am, what can I change about me that will help me solve the problems that I am having?" Change what you can, when you can. In other words, if you can make a change now, do it now. If you can't make it now, make it later—when you can.

Second, find time for yourself. Keep realistic work demands even if you do not give students all the assignments you think they should have. Our advice is that it is better to fill the time with quality teaching than to cover material. We also think that many teachers give way too much work in their first years, then slow this work down later on. Make sure there is a real reason for the assignments you will give. Don't give gratuitous material. Two reasons: (1) you don't need to and (2) guess who is responsible for marking it—you are!

Third, not every piece of curriculum material or lesson plan has to be original. During your first years, share. What you can't share, find. What you can't find, steal. Not every paper has to be read and graded. The teacher can't do it all. Learn to delegate. Some classroom administrative tasks can be done by students. You may even find a good student aide who is trustworthy and can help you grade objective tests. We would encourage you to consider buying a computer with a big hard drive for storage. This way all your typing, filing, and duplication is easy to access. School secretaries and the janitorial staff will be your best friends, but they must be treated well. They have a difficult job, and like anyone else they hate to be dumped on. But, they can and will help you. Delegate what you can to the school secretary. Collecting materials for lesson files can be delegated to the librarian. And parent helpers are an untapped resource. Elementary teachers use them, but, not secondary teachers. They should. Finally, remember that not every request has to be responded to with a yes. You are allowed to say NO. Repeat, you are allowed to say NO.

## A FINAL WORD

Finally, we would like to encourage you to work toward your own professional growth. There are some easy ways to grow as a teacher. First, remember that learning to teach is a lifelong quest. Think of yourself as a teacher. Remember the reasons why you became a teacher. Work hard. Second, attend seminars and workshops not to criticize others but to learn. Even if you might not totally agree with what other teachers say, consider what they do say. We see all too many teachers who seem to want to dump on everything. It's not a good attitude because it doesn't help you grow. Give people the benefit of the doubt. Listen with tolerance. Third, think of yourself not just as a teacher of your classroom but as a teacher who has much to share with other teachers all over the world. Attend regional, national, and even international conferences. We assure you, you will meet some great people—other teachers. You will also have some good times travelling and visiting.

Last, enjoy being a teacher. Be proud of what you do. In general, it's a great life.

## READINGS FOR EXTENSION AND ENRICHMENT

Charnock, Barbara, Kiley, Margaret (1995). *Concerns and Preferred Assistance Strategies of Beginning Middle and High School Teachers.* Paper presented at the Annual Meeting of the American Educational Research Association, San Francisco, CA. Reports on the causes of the high rates of attrition of beginning teachers and possible solutions to their exodus.

Gish, Steven C. (1994). *"Mr. Gish, May I Go to the Bathroom?" My First Year as a High School Teacher.* Port Angeles: WA: Deer Park Publications. This book presents the narrative of one educator's first year as a high school teacher

Lohr, Linda (1997). Assistance and Review: Helping New Teachers Get Started. *Teaching & Change, 6* (3), 295-313. Describes the Peer Assistance and Review Program, a collaborative, ongoing professional-assistance effort for beginning teachers in Columbus, Ohio's public schools.

Rosenberg, Michael S. Griffin, Cynthia C. Kilgore, Karen L. Carpenter, Stephanie L. (1997). Beginning Teachers in Special Education: A Model for Providing Individualized Support. *Teacher Education & Special Education, 20* (4), 301-21. Describes a model for providing individualized and comprehensive support for beginning special educators in the face of acute personnel shortages.

Rowley, James B. Hart, Patricia M. (2000). *High-Performance Mentoring: A Multimedia Program for Training Mentor Teachers.* Thousand Oaks, CA: Corwin Press, Inc. This book, designed to be used with a training workshop that helps veteran teachers be effective mentors to beginning teachers, provides instructions on how to facilitate a successful workshop.

Rust, Frances O'Connell (1999). Professional Conversations: New Teachers Explore Teaching through Conversation, Story, and Narrative. *Teaching & Teacher Education, 15* (4), 367-80. This study indicates the potential of conversation and storytelling to sustain teacher learning and inquiry.

Wolfe, Deborah (1999). Teaching: A Lifetime Commitment. *Kappa Delta Pi Record. 35 (2), 86-88.* This interview with Deborah Wolfe, an experienced teacher, examines her life as a teacher, what makes her a good teacher, what her first day of teaching was like, why there is such a demand for teachers, why the demand is an ongoing problem and her.

# CHAPTER 17

# The Rewards of a Teaching Career

*THEY fail and they alone, who have not striven.*

**-THOMAS BAILEY ALDRICH**

Here we are at the end of the book. Before we go we will leave you with one question. Maybe it's the most important question you will ask and answer for yourself: How will you find your joy in teaching?

We can't answer this question for you, but we can help you begin. We can also tell you without question that we think teaching is great and if we could think of anything better to do, we would quit teaching and do it. Don't get us wrong. Teaching isn't always great. But it's mostly great.

So, how will you find joy in teaching? You may not be able to answer immediately, but you probably have an idea why you decided to be a teacher in the first place. Are you interested in why other people choose to become teachers? A recent survey asked that very question of education students. Here are some of their answers. Most chose teaching because they wanted to make a positive difference in the lives of children; almost all chose teaching because they loved children; only about five percent named calendar considerations (having long holiday vacations) as important; almost all felt that teaching would allow them to express their creative abilities; and almost all saw teaching as an awesome responsibility. There were other interesting findings: only about one-fourth thought that teaching was a highly respected profession and almost all thought teachers were not adequately paid; but, they chose teaching anyway. More than half strongly felt that the rewards of teaching are not monetary; about one-third had a parent who was a teacher; and more than half were influenced by one or more former teachers. How do these reasons sound to you?

One reason for revisiting the question of why people choose to teach is that we hope you will not forget why you chose to become a teacher. If you are similar to others, your reasons are based on internal, not external, rewards. Although we would wish that teachers received high salaries and high status, this isn't so. We are convinced that it is the internal rewards that will keep you refreshed and restored as a teacher.

As we said earlier, most people already know that the rewards of teaching are not external. Still, the vocation of teaching is being embraced by some of the best and brightest people in society. However, some very competent people avoid the teaching profession because it lacks economic and prestige incentives. Some of our colleagues lament this fact; but, we don't. Quite the opposite. Although it may sound a bit odd, there are parts of us that hope teaching never has many extrinsic rewards. We think

> **"A teacher affects eternity; he can never tell where his influence stops."**
> *- Henry Adams*

that teachers are both called to be teachers and educated to be teachers. We want people who really want to be teachers to be teachers. Anyone who goes into teaching for the money or status should seek a more appropriate occupation. We also believe that the more teachers come to rely on intrinsic rewards the better off they will be.

Teaching is often portrayed as a negative job, devoid of any extrinsic rewards. You will not receive a good salary (you don't get paid very much), high status (the status of teachers has declined in the past decade), a heavy work schedule (teachers always take much work home), lack of flexibility (day after day you do the same thing), and a lack of power (power is seen as an extrinsic reward in most occupations but is seldom mentioned by teachers).

Our answer: we feed our families now and we did when we were real teachers. Often we are told that what we do makes a difference to people's lives. We care about our work and we believe it's important. It's work we like to do and when we are away for a long time we want to get back at it. We may teach the same classes, but we learn new things and we meet a wide variety of people day after day. We get to do things, more or less, the way we want to. As long as we do our jobs well we seldom get hassled. We have great freedom.

Who's right? Us or the critics? That, you'll have to find out for yourselves.

We know many older teachers who quit because they just can't take it. It's not that they were poor teachers; many have just run out of steam. Still, many experienced teachers remain in the profession. Some have positive reasons (they continue to love teaching); some have negative reasons (they have no other job they can do). Often, the quality of the staff they are working with or the strengths of their friendships with other teachers or with their students encourages many teachers to stay in the profession.

The best teachers we know say that the intrinsic rewards make teaching more of a calling than a job. This is the reason they stay. Research suggests that it is only when intrinsic rewards diminish that extrinsic concerns like salary and working conditions become truly significant. Unfortunately, as soon as extrinsic rewards become the reason for staying in teaching, teachers usually quit - either by leaving the classroom or by staying in the classroom but not working up to full potential. If money is not the prime motivation for the hard work of teachers, teachers can encourage each other to regard their work as professionals, to encourage creative instruction, and to gain a sense of community. These are some of the true rewards of teaching. They are all intrinsic.

One intrinsic reward we seldom hear people talking about is that most students are really neat people. We believe that most teachers think as we do. They feel good when their students achieve. They also feel a strong sense of attachment to the young people in their classes. Greatest among the rewards of teaching is the affection that moves back and forth, quite naturally really, between teachers and their students. Mostly we are working with people who like each other.

Teachers work to improve the whole class, but often find their greatest rewards in the successes of individual students. Teachers also share a great deal with each other. They are, or could be, colleagues in the best sense. They work to support each other, and they enjoy support and praise from colleagues for work well done. This collegial support can be particularly important in schools where rewarding interactions with students are minimal.

Another reward of teaching is the opportunity for continual learning and professional improvement. In addition to money, teachers find that personal status for a job well done, working hours compatible with family life, a sense of affiliation, autonomy, responsibility, and opportunities for creativity and psychological rewards are the motivating incentives of the teaching profession. Teachers gain internal rewards and teaching efficacy, plus they tend to work in good environments, especially when compared to other occupations. Most of the schools we know, unless ruined by administrators, other teachers, or nastiness from outside sources, are good places to work.

Sometimes, finding rewards in teaching is not easy. Teaching, like most work, is a mix of the good and the bad. For example, a recent survey reported some interesting findings: more than half of the teachers frequently or continuously received tangible rewards from teaching that make them enthusiastic about their jobs; most teachers never wished they had chosen another vocation; most teachers indicate that they had higher expectations for student performance than two years ago, and they believed students had increased their abilities and desires to learn; about one of four teachers were encouraged by opportunities for advancement; more than half of the teachers often helped students with non-academic problems; and more than half received support and encouragement from their principals. In general, these teachers had a positive view of their own work.

If you choose to become a classroom teacher, there are some cautions we would like to make. Because teaching is often devalued and misrepresented, their earning potential is lower than that of other professions. As well, in most schools, especially large urban high schools, teachers are too often colleagues in name only. This second point describes the way things are, not the way they could be. For example, some schools foster collegial relationships among teachers. And when schools are organized to support such teacher collaboration, the benefits are substantial. The point is, you can choose to shape your school in positive ways for both yourself and your students. But you must choose to do so.

Teachers are no different from other humans. They are, and generally love to be, social. The ability to build a community where teachers work together is one important reward in teaching. To make teacher collaboration possible and effective, there are two fundamental and crucial conditions - interdependence and opportunity. Because teachers' main motivations and rewards come from the very work of teaching, the more teachers can work interdependently with one another the more easily they can reap the rewards of teaching. Making joint work a worthwhile investment of time and resources is a key to finding joy in teaching. Again, you must choose to do so.

> "What office is there which involves more responsibility which requires more qualifications and which ought, therefore, to be more honourable, than that of teaching."
>
> *- Harriet Martineau*

Working together will not occur where not encouraged or where it is made prohibitively costly in organizational, political, or personal terms. Helping teacher collaboration to work requires endorsements and rewards for collaborative efforts, school-level reorganization into teams to stimulate cooperative work, the willingness to give latitude to teachers for influence on matters of curriculum and instruction, enough time for planning periods and implementation, training and assistance, and the support of quality materials and equipment. Since school policy can be shaped by teachers, we encourage you to work toward these ends.

One study explored how two secondary teachers developed healthy, caring bonds with their students and how they nurtured healthy emotional and social development in young people. Findings revealed that the two teachers were committed to fostering students' social and emotional development and recognized that interactions with students influenced student self-esteem and self-worth. The teachers studied had distinct styles for bonding with students - one used quality one-to-one time with meaningful or responsive dialogue and the other used self-disclosure through dialogue. Intrapersonal qualities like genuineness, inner locus of control, flexibility and adaptability, humor, enthusiasm, and non judgmental stance all proved to be important factors in building positive relationships with students. Interpersonal skills like communication, empowerment, problem-solving, conflict resolution, and respect were also positive motivations for these positive relationships. The teachers' sources of revitalization were identified as the rewards of teaching, coping mechanisms, and support from the workplace.

Simply put, there is a great deal of enjoyment in creating good teaching activities. Some teachers gain joy from conducting a carefully planned lesson. Others get satisfaction from creating a stimulating classroom environment.

Where is the joy in teaching? That, you'll have to find out for yourselves. We know personally that it is there, and we hope that you find teaching just as rewarding as we do. Write us and tell us how you are doing. If you do, we get another reward for teaching.

## READINGS FOR EXTENSION AND ENRICHMENT

Eshelman, Darla, Nelson, Joy (1994). A Teacher's Guide to First-Year Survival. *Music Educators Journal, 81* (1), 29-31,47. Presents eight guidelines for surviving and enjoying the first year of teaching.

Hill, Lynn T. (1995). Helping Teachers Love Their Work. *Child Care Information Exchange, 104* (30), 32-34. Examines three reasons teachers leave their profession and approaches for helping them to love their work.

Kuzmic, Jeff (1994). A Beginning Teacher's Search for Meaning: Teacher Socialization, Organizational Literacy, and Empowerment. *Teaching & Teacher Education, 10* (1), 15-27. Examines the socialization of a beginning kindergarten teacher as a means for better understanding the socialization process and the implications for teacher education.

O'Brien, Pat McDonald (1999). Finding My Place at the Table. *Voices From the Middle, 6* (3), 30-32. Observes that teaching today is a major challenge as teachers attempt to sift through everything that confronts them and as they constantly struggle with conflict while trying to address the complex dilemmas facing them daily in their classrooms.

Paschke, Meredith (1996). Things College Never Taught Me (New Teachers). *English Journal, 85* (2), 85-86. Describes a first-year teacher's experience teaching unruly seventh graders and how she has learned, to a degree, to smile and to be patient, and find consolation in those students who have written to her to express how much she has helped them through her teaching and counseling.

Stanish, Bob (1994). Keeping Teaching Alive. *Gifted Child Today, 17* (1), 27-28,30-31,41. This discussion of the need to keep young and talented teachers in teaching describes two projects in which a teacher took risks to create innovative learning activities for gifted intermediate grade students.

# Quotation Sources

Preface    Hopi - as quoted in Zona, Guy A., *The Soul Would Have No Rainbow if the Eyes Had No Tears and Other Native American Proverbs.* New York, NY: Touchstone (1994).

Preface    Armiger Barclay - *The Kingmakers.* Boston: Small, Maynard and Co. (1907).

Page 1    Henry David Thoreau - *Journal* (Oct. 1850). Princeton, NJ: Princeton University Press (1981).

Page 3    L. Rubin - *Journal of Teacher Education,* 40(6) (1989).

Page 5    Jean Paul Sartre - as quoted in E. Dale, *The Educator's Quote Book* . Bloomington, IN: Phi Delta Kappan Educational Foundation (1984).

Page 7    Source unknown.

Page 8    Charles F. Kettering - *Seed for Thought* (1949).

Page 11    Publilius Syrus - source unknown.

Page 13    Harold Hulbert - *Reader's Digest* (1949).

Page 14    Ralph Hodgson - *The Skylark and Other Poems.* London: C. Fendon (1958).

Page 16    Frederick Langbridge - *A Cluster of Quiet Thoughts.* London: Religious Tract Society (1896).

Page 18    Antoine de Saints-Exupery - *The Wisdom of the Sand.* New York: Harcourt, Brace (1950).

Page 21    Donald D. Quinn - as quoted in E. Dale, *The Educator's Quote Book.* Bloomington, IN: Phi Delta Kappan Educational Foundation (1984).

Page 23    Pogo - source unknown.

Page 25   Charles Brower - *Advertising Age* (Aug. 1O, 1959).

Page 29   Austin O'Malley - *Keystone of Thoughts* (1914-15).

Page 31   Source unknown.

Page 32   J. Petit-Senn - *Conceits and Caprices* . New York: Hurd and Houghton (1869).

Page 35   Robert F. Capon - *Bed and Board* (1965).

Page 36   C. J. Friedrich - *An Introduction to Political Theory* (1967).

Page 39   Vernon Saunders Law - *This Week* (Aug. 14, 1960).

Page 41   Aeschylus - *Prometheus Bound*, In.35 (c490 B.C.). Oxford; Clarendon (1883).

Page 42   Gordon W. Allport - *Personality and Social Encounter: Prejudice in Modern Perspective*. Boston: Beacon Press (1960).

Page 45   Old New England saying.

Page 47   Henry Wadsworth Longfellow - *Driftwood: Table Talk*. London: W. Kent and Co. (late D. Bogue) (1858).

Page 49   Albert Einstein - motto for the Astronomy Building, Pasadena Junior College.

Page 51   Kahil Gibran - *The Prophet: On Children*. New York: A.A. Knopf (1923).

Page 52   Source unknown.

Page 55   George A. Miller - as quoted in E. Dale, *The Educator's Quote Book*. Bloomington, IN: Phi Delta Kappan Educational Foundation (1984).

Page 56   Source unknown.

Page 58   Source unknown

Page 63   William Alexander - *Doomsday: The Ninth Hour* (1614).

Page 65   Source Unknown.

Page 66   Heywood Broun - *Sitting in the World*. New York and London: G. Putman's Sons (1924).

Page 68   Chuang-tzu - *Philosophy* xi (4th-3rd cent. B.C.).

Page 71   Elbert Hubbard - *Note Book*. New York: W.H. Wise and Company (1927).

Page 72   Henry Ward Beecher - *Proverbs from Plymouth Pulpit: Children*. New York: D. Appleton and Company (1887).

Page 73   Lord Avebury and John Lubbock - as quoted in E. Dale, *The Educator's Quote Book*. Bloomington, IN: Phi Delta Kappan Educational Foundation (1984).

Page 77   John F. Kennedy - Address at San Diego State College, June 16, 1963.

Page 78   Sa'di - *Tales from the Gulistan*. London: P. Allan (1928).

Page 80   George Bernard Shaw - *The Intelligent Woman's Guide to Socialism and Capitalism*. New York: Bretano's (1928).

Page 84   Emily Dickinson - *Complete Poems*, Edited by Thomas Johnson. Boston: Little Brown (1960).

Page 87   Robert G. Ingersoll - *Liberty in Literature* (1890).

Page 89   John Galsworthy - *Swan Song*. London: Heinemann (1928).

Page 90 John Amos Comenius - *The Great Didactic*. London: A.C. Black (1921).

Page 93 Logan Pearsal Smith - as quoted in E. Dale, *The Educator's Quote Book*. Bloomington, IN: Phi Delta Kappan Educational Foundation (1984).

Page 94 Source unknown.

Page 97 Plato - as quoted in E. Dale, *The Educator's Quote Book*. Bloomington, IN: Phi Delta Kappan Educational Foundation (1984).

Page 101 Source unknown.

Page 103 Publilius Syrus - *Sententiae* (c.43 B.C.).

Page 105 Edgar Dale - *The Educator's Quote Book*. Bloomington, IN: Phi Delta Kappan Educational Foundation (1984).

Page 108 Source unknown.

Page 110 Danish proverb.

Page 113 Charles Synge Christopher Bowen - *Lecture on Education*. (1835-94).

Page 115 E.M. Forster - *New York Times*, Nov. 24, 1963.

Page 117 Richard Livingstone - *On Education*. Cambridge: The University Press (1944).

Page 118 Johann Herbart - *Collected Works* (1850-52): *Brief Encyclopedia of Practical Philosophy*.

Page 121 Bertrand Russell - *Principles of Social Reconstruction: Education* (1916).

Page 123 Alfred North Whithead - *The Aims of Education*. New York: New American Library (1929).

Page 125 Ruth Gordon - *Over Twenty-One* (1949).

Page 126 Stephen Leacock - *My Discovery of England: Oxford As I See It*. London: John Lane (1922).

Page 129 Charles Caleb Colton - *Lacon*, 170 (1820-22).

Page 131 Publilius Syrus - *Sententiae*, no. 586 (c,43 B.C.).

Page 133 Margaret Eldredge Howell - *Wormwood* (1893-1946).

Page 135 Fritz Peris - *Omni* (Nov. 1977).

Page 136 Source unknown.

Page 140 William James - *The Principles of Psychology*, II. 369, (1890).

Page 143 Dagobed D. Runes - source unknown.

Page 145 Richard Arends - *Learning to Teach*. New York: McGraw Hill. (1991).

Page 146 Alice Freeman Palmer - source unknown.

Page 148 Milton Caniff - as quoted in E. Dale, *The Educator's Quote Book*. Bloomington, IN: Phi Delta Kappan Educational Foundation (1984).

Page 150 James Russell Lowell - as quoted in E. Dale, *The Educator's Quote Book*. Bloomington, IN: Phi Delta Kappan Educational Foundation (1984).

Page 152 Ken Jacknicke - personal conversation (1990).

Page 155 Michael Soule, in D. Western & M.C. Pearle, *Conservation for the 21st Century* (1989).

Page 156 Mark Twain, http://quotations.about.com/arts/quotations/library/db/blauth_twain_bks.htm

Page 159 Isaac Asimov, http://www.feist.com/~degood/computer.html

Page 160 Association of American Colleges, Report, "Integrity in the College Curriculum" (Feb. 1985).

Page 163 Prince Philip, *Men, Machines and Sacred Cows* (1984).

Page 164 Abraham Maslow, Source unknown.

Page 166 Pablo Picasso, http://www.feist.com/~degood/computer.html

Page 169 Beryl Bainbridge - *Injury Time* (1978).

Page 171 F. Scott Fitzgerald - *Flappers and Philosophers: Bernice Bobs Her Hair.* New York: Scribner's Sons (1920).

Page 173 Ovid - as quoted in E. Dale, *The Educator's Quote Book.* Bloomington, IN: Phi Delta Kappan Educational Foundation (1984).

Page 174 James M. Barrie - as quoted in E. Dale, *The Educator's Quote Book.* Bloomington, IN: Phi Delta Kappan Educational Foundation (1984).

Page 177 George Bernard Shaw - as quoted in E. Dale, *The Educator's Quote Book.* Bloomington, IN: Phi Delta Kappan Educational Foundation (1984).

Page 180 Elbert Hubbard - *Note Book.* New York: W.H. Wise & Co. (1927).

Page 183 Carl Gustav Jung - *Psychological Reflections*, Jolanda Jacobi and R.F. Hull (Eds.) (1970).

Page 184 Jerome Cramet - *Time* (June 16, 1980).

Page 185 Ezra Pound - *ABC of Reading.* London: G. Routledge & Sons, Ltd. (1934).

Page 188 Cardinal Newman - as quoted in E. Dale, *The Educator's Quote Book.* Bloomington, IN: Phi Delta Kappan Educational Foundation (1984).

Page 189 Mark Twain - *Pudd'nhead Wilson's New Calendar* (1897).

Page 193 Thomas Bailey Aldrich - *Enamored Architect of Airy Rhyme* (c.1880).

Page 194 Henry Adams - *The Education of Henry Adams* (1907).

Page 196 Harriet Martineau - *Society in America, III: Women* (1837).

# Subject Index